ROBIN HOOD

The Legend. Re-written.

by Carl Grose

SAMUEL FRENCH

Copyright © 2023 by Carl Grose
Cover design: feastcreative.com. Photography: Oliver Rosser
All Rights Reserved

ROBIN HOOD is fully protected under the copyright laws of the British Commonwealth, including Canada, the United States of America, and all other countries of the Copyright Union. All rights, including professional and amateur stage productions, recitation, lecturing, public reading, motion picture, radio broadcasting, television, online/digital production, and the rights of translation into foreign languages are strictly reserved.

ISBN 978-0-573-00031-7

concordtheatricals.co.uk
concordtheatricals.com

FOR AMATEUR PRODUCTION ENQUIRIES

UNITED KINGDOM AND WORLD
EXCLUDING NORTH AMERICA
licensing@concordtheatricals.co.uk
020-7054-7298

Each title is subject to availability from Concord Theatricals, depending upon country of performance.

CAUTION: Professional and amateur producers are hereby warned that *ROBIN HOOD* is subject to a licensing fee. The purchase, renting, lending or use of this book does not constitute a licence to perform this title(s), which licence must be obtained from the appropriate agent prior to any performance. Performance of this title(s) without a licence is a violation of copyright law and may subject the producer and/or presenter of such performances to penalties. Both amateurs and professionals considering a production are strongly advised to apply to the appropriate agent before starting rehearsals, advertising, or booking a theatre. A licensing fee must be paid whether the title is presented for charity or gain and whether or not admission is charged.

This work is published by Samuel French, an imprint of Concord Theatricals Ltd.

Professional rights in this title are controlled by The Agency (London) Ltd, 24 Pottery Lane, London W11 4LN.

No one shall make any changes in this title for the purpose of production. No part of this book may be reproduced, stored in a retrieval system, scanned, uploaded, or transmitted in any form, by any means, now known or yet to be invented, including mechanical, electronic, digital, photocopying, recording, videotaping, or otherwise, without the prior written permission of the publisher. No one shall share this title, or part of this title, to any social media or file hosting websites.

The moral right of Carl Grose to be identified as author of this work has been asserted in accordance with Section 77 of the Copyright, Designs and Patents Act 1988.

USE OF COPYRIGHTED MUSIC

A licence issued by Concord Theatricals to perform this play does not include permission to use the incidental music specified in this publication. In the United Kingdom: Where the place of performance is already licensed by the PERFORMING RIGHT SOCIETY (PRS) a return of the music used must be made to them. If the place of performance is not so licensed then application should be made to PRS for Music (www.prsformusic.com). A separate and additional licence from PHONOGRAPHIC PERFORMANCE LTD (www.ppluk.com) may be needed whenever commercial recordings are used. Outside the United Kingdom: Please contact the appropriate music licensing authority in your territory for the rights to any incidental music.

USE OF COPYRIGHTED THIRD-PARTY MATERIALS

Licensees are solely responsible for obtaining formal written permission from copyright owners to use copyrighted third-party materials (e.g., artworks, logos) in the performance of this play and are strongly cautioned to do so. If no such permission is obtained by the licensee, then the licensee must use only original materials that the licensee owns and controls. Licensees are solely responsible and liable for clearances of all third-party copyrighted materials, and shall indemnify the copyright owners of the play(s) and their licensing agent, Concord Theatricals Ltd., against any costs, expenses, losses and liabilities arising from the use of such copyrighted third-party materials by licensees.

IMPORTANT BILLING AND CREDIT REQUIREMENTS

If you have obtained performance rights to this title, please refer to your licensing agreement for important billing and credit requirements.

ROBIN HOOD was commissioned by and first performed at Regent's Park Open Air Theatre, London on 23 June 2023. The cast was as follows:

MARIAN	Ellen Robertson
WOODNUT	Dumile Lindiwe Sibanda
THE BALLADEER / JENNY MUCH	Nandi Bhebhe
LITTLE JOAN	Charlotte Beaumont
MARY TUCK	Elexi Walker
WILL SCATLOCKE	Samuel Gosrani
BOB MUCH	Dave Fishley
BALDWYN	Alex Mugnaioni
SIMPKINS	Katherine Manners
THE KING	Paul Hunter
BETTY	Stephanie Marion Fayerman
GISBURNE	Ira Mandela Siobhan
BRASSWILT / ROBIN HOOD 1 / GUARD / VILLAGER	TJ Holmes
BRICKBROKE / ROBIN HOOD 2 / GUARD / VILLAGER	Shaun Yusuf McKee
BONEWEATHER / ROBIN HOOD 3 / GUARD / VILLAGER	Simon Oskarsson

MUSICIANS . . . . Amena Alicia El-kindy, Taya Ming, Marta Miranda

CREATIVE TEAM

DIRECTOR	Melly Still
COMPOSER, MUSICAL SUPERVISOR & ADDITIONAL LYRICS	Jenny Moore
SET DESIGNER	Chiara Stephenson
COSTUME DESIGNER	Samuel Wyer
LIGHTING DESIGNER	Zoe Spurr
SOUND DESIGNER	Emma Laxton
MOVEMENT DIRECTOR	Mike Ashcroft
ILLUSION DESIGNER	John Bulleid
MUSICAL DIRECTOR	Joley Cragg
ASSOCIATE DIRECTOR	Poppy Franziska
ASSOCIATE SET DESIGNER	Mauricio Elorriaga, Olivia Walters
PROPS SUPERVISOR	Poppy Morris for Propworks
COSTUME SUPERVISOR	Sabia Smith
CASTING DIRECTOR	Polly Jerrold

VOICE & TEXT DIRECTOR .... Jeanette Nelson
DRAMATURG .... Deirdre O'Halloran
SEASON ASSOCIATE: INTIMACY SUPPORT ...... Ingrid Mackinnon

COMPANY STAGE MANAGER .... Lou Ballard
DEPUTY STAGE MANAGER .... Sophia "Saf" Horrocks
ASSISTANT STAGE MANAGER .... Roma Radford
PRODUCTION MANAGER .... Chris Easton

REGENT'S PARK OPEN AIR THEATRE

Established in 1932, the multi-award-winning Regent's Park Open Air Theatre is one of the largest independent, not-for-profit producing theatres in London. Situated in the beautiful surroundings of a Royal Park, the theatre plays a unique role in the UK's cultural landscape and has a worldwide reputation for creating popular, enriching and unexpected theatre that provides a lens into the here and now.

Led by Joint Chief Executives Timothy Sheader (Artistic Director) and James Pidgeon (Executive Director), the theatre welcomes over 140,000 visitors every year. Recent productions include *Lord of the Flies*, *The Seagull*, *Peter Pan*, *Henry V*, *On The Town*, *To Kill a Mockingbird*, *As You Like It*, *Little Shop of Horrors*, *A Midsummer Night's Dream*, *Evita*, *Romeo and Juliet*, *Carousel*, *Legally Blonde*, *101 Dalmatians*, *Antigone* and *Once On This Island*.

Co-productions include *The Turn of the Screw* and *Hansel and Gretel* (with English National Opera; *Running Wild* (with Chichester Festival Theatre) and *Anansi the Spider* (with Unicorn Theatre). Productions have transferred to the West End and North America, where the theatre's Olivier and Evening Standard award-winning *Jesus Christ*

Superstar is currently touring. A UK tour of *Jesus Christ Superstar* will commence in September 2023.

In 2023, Regent's Park Open Air Theatre presented two new commissioned works: an adaptation of Ben Okri's new fairytale *Every Leaf A Hallelujah*, adapted by Chinonyerem Odimba for everyone aged 4+, and a thrilling new take on the classic tale, *Robin Hood: The Legend. Rewritten.* by Carl Grose. The theatre also produced work for children and families throughout the entirety of the 2023 season, including *The Tempest* re-imagined for everyone aged six and over in a co-production with the Unicorn Theatre.

For more information, visit openairtheatre.com.

CHARACTERS

MARIAN
WOODNUT
THE BALLADEER / JENNY MUCH
LITTLE JOAN
MARY TUCK
WILL SCATLOCKE
BOB MUCH
BALDWYN
SIMPKINS
THE KING
BETTY
GISBURNE
THREE ROBIN HOODS
BARONS BONEWEATHER, BRASSWILT & BRICKBROKE

And, where we can:

VILLAGERS
THE SHERIFF'S MEN
A CHEST FULL OF SEVERED FINGERS

TIME AND SETTING

The play is set somewhere between Mediaeval and Contemporary. This is not a historical retelling. It exists in its own folk tale world. We're not in Sherwood. We're in the ancient Green Wood of Old England.

There are several locations – the castle, the village, the forest, the underground – that sometimes play concurrently. There are hard cuts and fast edits. Like in a film. Your playing space, and hence your stage design, should be fluid and fleet and fast. Scene changes will kill the flow.

A Note on The Balladeer

The balladeer was a stable of the Robin Hood form back in the day. It's how these tales were originally communicated, stories told through songs called ballads. I've used that convention here, but how you want her to communicate her text (be it sung, spoken, sung-spoken or a mix of all three) is entirely up to you.

AUTHOR'S NOTE

There's so much of the Robin Hood legend that still delights us to this day. We love the cunning, cleverness and courage of the outsiders in the woods as they over-throw the powers-that-be. Who doesn't love the idea of robbing of the rich to give to the poor (except the rich)? We love the adventure, the romance, the iconic characters and moments... all of this is contained within in epic fashion. The only element that seemed slightly hackneyed in approaching this new version was the dear old man himself.

And so, I've retold the story, but without him. Kind of. There's still a flash of green tights (how could there not be?) but he isn't the main character by any stretch. Here, he's relegated to the side-lines and made to watch (indeed, he even learns a thing or two). The main character is a young girl called Woodnut. The story is experienced through her eyes and it's hoped she brings a fresh perspective to the tale.

There's still the dastardly sheriff, Marian, Tuck and Will Scarlet, but no Nottingham, Sherwood or Prince John. This is a subversive origin story, what 'actually happened' before the Elizabethan playwright Anthony Munday turned Hood from working class hero to disinherited earl and Disney turned him into a talking fox. This is a folktale for our times. There's no historical connections at all. But it does, I hope, provide a wildly thrilling contemporary take on the story. It's about England. It questions who owns this land and who owns this country's myths, stories and culture. The quick answer is... we all do.

This is the story of the fight to get them back.

Whether you're reading it, or mounting a new production, I hope you have fun.

And let those arrows fly!

Carl Grose

ACKNOWLEDGEMENTS

A huge thank you to Mandy and Arthur Ray, and to Ronald Hutton, James Thompson, Steven Green, Mike Shepherd, Stu Barker, Julia Kreitman, Tim Sheader, James Pigeon, Lauren King, Arianne Brooks, Minnie Cunningham, Nic Wass, the amazing Regent's Park crew, The brilliant Robin Hood Creative Team, incredible cast for their insightful and fabulous contributions, the fearless Poppy Franziska, the sublime Jenny Moore and the living legend that is Melly Still... Huzzah!

PART ONE

(Before us, an England of two halves; a kingdom divided.)

(From the top down, the **KING** *sits in a castle turret, on his throne. He drowsily sips tea from a cup.* **BALDWYN**, *the sheriff, bows and prepares a decree for the* **KING**. *Elsewhere, his wife* **MARIAN** *sits, drinking from a goblet and* **SIMPKINS**, *Baldwyn's no-nonsense assistant, hovers nearby. Below, in the village, we find an assortment of beleaguered souls including* **BETTY**, *the village elder,* **BOB MUCH**, *the miller, who slowly turns a handle to grind the wheat he hasn't got, and his daughter,* **WOODNUT**, *a child of ten, who sweeps.)*

(Enter the **BALLADEER** *from the forest. She is our storyteller.)*

BALLADEER. So, you get the picture?

Does this look familiar?

A kingdom cracked

Right down the centre...

Another dawn, another day

For this broke-down village

Between palace and forest

Where they're scared the sheriff's men

Might come again...

Woodsmoke and fear hang in the air

Eyes cast down to the hard stony ground

And whilst the rich and royal up there thrive –

BALDWYN. Your majesty…

KING. I'm sure I don't know what I'm signing half the time, Anthony.

>   *(The **KING** signs a decree.)*

BALLADEER. These poor souls hang by their nails to survive!

EVERYONE. Another dawn, another day

Another dawn, another –

>   *(**BALDWYN** and **SIMPKINS** enter the village. She blows a horrible horn. Everyone stops, fearful.)*

SIMPKINS. Stop singing, you lot! Sheriff Baldwyn has something to say!

BALDWYN. *(Holds up the papers.)* I have here a new law, the royal signature freshly upon it. All will make their contribution to the royal coffers today. Failure to pay will result in severe punishment. No excuses, no exceptions. Thank you, Simpkins.

>   *(A ripple of dismay goes through the **VILLAGERS**. **SIMPKINS** starts going from door to door, collecting from those who have nothing. Two of the **SHERIFF'S MEN** [brutes with bats] join her.)*

SIMPKINS. Knock, knock! Tax please? Thank you.

Knock, knock! Tax please? Thank you…

>   *(**WOODNUT** watches on.)*

Knock, knock! Tax please?

> (**BETTY**, *a village elder, answers the door.*)

BETTY. Hello dear.

SIMPKINS. Tax please.

BETTY. I got nuthin for you, I'm afraid.

SIMPKINS. The king demands one quarter of your earnings, old woman.

BETTY. Then the King can take one quarter of bugger all.

SIMPKINS. *(Shouts.)* Take her away!

> (*Poor* **BETTY** *is dragged off – but not without a fight.*)

BALDWYN. An example must be made! Good work, Simpkins. Next?

SIMPKINS. Knock, knock. Tax please?

> (**WOODNUT** *runs home to her father,* **BOB**.)

WOODNUT. Sheriff's come for his taxes! What we gonna do, dad?

BOB. We've nuthin to give them. What can we do?

WOODNUT. We better think of summin quick cus they'll drag us to the Hanging Post for scaldings and gougings and God knows what else. They've already taken poor old Betty.

> *(Beat.)*

If mum were here she'd stand and fight.

BOB. As she did in life, Woodnut. And look where that got her.

SIMPKINS. *(Outside.)* Knock, knock! Tax please!

WOODNUT. What should we do? Dad?

> (But **BOB** is in a daze. **WOODNUT** realises she's on her own.)

BALLADEER. She's about to face the enemy

And these goading beasts have jagged teeth

Lash down that wayward tongue, girl

And pretend you feel no grief...

SIMPKINS. BOOMBOOMBOOM! Much the miller? Open up!

> (**WOODNUT** appears at the door.)

Tax!

WOODNUT. My father's been struck down by a terrible sadness.

SIMPKINS. Then go fetch your mother and she can pay me.

WOODNUT. My mother is dead. That's why he's in such deep despair.

SIMPKINS. So how do you intend to pay?

WOODNUT. Dad'll teach me the ropes soon enough. Then I can work. Then I can pay. I just need more time.

SIMPKINS. More time?!

BALDWYN. Problem, Simpkins?

SIMPKINS. It's the old 'dead mother' routine, sir.

BALDWYN. Allow me...

> (He barges his way in. **WOODNUT** stares daggers at the sheriff. **BALDWYN** scopes the place out, glancing at **BOB**.)

Tell me child, when did your mother die?

WOODNUT. When you gave the order to storm our village.

BALDWYN. Ah. Last week.

WOODNUT. She was struck by an arrow fired by one of your men.

BALDWYN. If she was one of those hooligans attacking the palace, she got what was coming to her.

WOODNUT. She was protecting the forest and you killed her for it.

BALDWYN. That is a very serious accusation, child.

WOODNUT. S'a very serious crime, sheriff.

BALDWYN. Slander is against the law.

WOODNUT. What isn't, these days?

BALDWYN. O, I can think of a few more things yet.

>   *(To* **SIMPKINS**.*)* Take her to the Hanging Post and cut out her tongue.

>   *(***WOODNUT** *is seized.)*

BOB. Wait. I'll pay.

BALDWYN. Ah! There we are, you see, Simpkins? The melancholy miller has miraculously located the king's payment, which means you get to keep your tongue, little adder!

>   *(***BALDWYN** *watches a broken* **BOB** *open his satchel to find money.* **WOODNUT** *goes to him.)*

SIMPKINS. Masterfully done, sir. Textbook extraction.

BALDWYN. Apply pressure where it hurts, Simpkins. They soon reveal themselves for the crooks they are. We make a good team, you and I.

BOB. *(Whispers.)* Woodnut? You must run.

WOODNUT. Run? But where's the money?

BOB. Head for the forest. Find your mother's grave. Remember what she taught you? About how to find your way in the woods?

WOODNUT. *(Remembers.)* Tickle for trout, flint for fire...

BOB. Take this.

> *(He hands her the satchel of things, but not before taking something for himself.)*

WOODNUT. Mum's forest things?

BOB. She'd want you to have them. Now, run –

WOODNUT. Shall I meet you there?

BOB. And don't look back.

WOODNUT. But dad... I'll meet you there?

BALDWYN. Come on, Much. Give us what we're owed.

BOB. *(Steeling himself.)* With pleasure...

> *(**BOB** reveals he has a knife and swings for **BALDWYN**.)*

SIMPKINS. Look out, sir!

> *(**SIMPKINS** throws herself in the way of the blade. In a mad flurry, **BOB** slashes her cheek in the chaos. Sheriff's men roughly disarm **BOB** and force him to his knees.)*

BALDWYN. Attempted murder on an officer of the crown? That's a hanging offence, man.

> *(**SIMPKINS** twists Bob's arm behind his back.)*

WOODNUT. No!

BOB. Woodnut! Run!

> *(**WOODNUT** tears out of the house and heads for the forest.)*

BALDWYN. Let her go. The forest will devour her.

BOB. She knows how to befriend wolves.

BALDWYN. O, there's worse than wolves in those woods, miller. She won't last five minutes when the outlaws catch a whiff of her tender young flesh...the desperate, the deranged, the dregs of humanity.

> (**BOB** *tries to go for him again, but he's pinned.*)

SIMPKINS. Take him away!

> (*Before* **BOB** *can protest he is dragged out.*)

BALDWYN. Blamed me for killing her mother? Whatever next, Simpkins? How's the cheek?

SIMPKINS. Just a scratch, sir.

BALDWYN. (*To the* **VILLAGERS**.) It pains me to uphold such penalties but an example must be made!

> (*To the village.*)

The king's peace be with you!

> (*Suddenly, music crashes in [Erich Korngold's soaring strings] and –)*

> (*Enter* **ROBIN HOOD**.)

> (*He's your classic Errol Flynn type. Feather in cap. Green tights. Arms akimbo.*)

ROBIN HOOD. Have no fear, poor villagers, you need not hang your heads! I am here! Robin Hood! The outlaw king! Lord of the Wood! Protector of the poor! Scourge of the greedy!

BALLADEER. Sorry. Can I help you?

ROBIN HOOD. Why no, goodly maid, tis I who have come to help *you.*

> *(Sings.)*

THE NOBLEST HERO, THE LORD OF THE WOOD
I'M ROBIN, I'M ROBIN, I'M ROBIN THE –

BALLADEER. Actually, we're doing something slightly different today.

ROBIN HOOD. Different?

BALLADEER. We're telling the *true* story.

ROBIN HOOD. And there is none truer than I! Where is my bow? My quiver? My quarterstaff? They should be here... Little John, that trickster!

BALLADEER. What I mean is, we don't need you today. Put your feet up, take a seat and enjoy from there.

ROBIN HOOD. Look here, if you don't let me do my job, I shall be forced to settle this through brute strength and may the best man win! Huzzah!

> *(Sings.)*

FAL-LA-LA! FOLL-DEE-DOO-DAY! FOLL-DEE-DAY-DOO!
FAL-LA-LA, LA, LA! WAH-HAY, NONNY-NOO!
OF ALL ENGLISH LEGENDS THAT EVER WERE TOLD
THE GREATEST OF ALL WAS OF ROBIN THE –

> *(The Balladeer's band creep in with a sack and try to bag him.* **ROBIN HOOD** *is chased off.)*

> *(Forest.)*

> *(***WOODNUT*** tears through the trees and emerges into clearing where her mother's grave lies. It is a broken mill stone with a heart scratched into it.* **WOODNUT** *falls down before it, breathless and scared.)*

BALLADEER. This shady glade

Her mother's favourite place

This humble grave

A cracked millstone to mark

The ground where she lay

Bones and roots, bones and earth

Yield, child – here in the wood's heart

Yield, child...

> *(Somewhere, a strange bird cries.* **WOODNUT** *looks about the place.)*

WOODNUT. *(Remembering her lessons.)* Yield before Nature, she will respect you

Take too much, she will bite back

Don't drink water from still silent pools

> *(She starts to build a small fire.)*

Always build shelter facing windward

Deadwood moss makes the best pillows

Dry sticks, never wet

Always carry –

> *(She looks in the bag and finds –)*

Flint and steel!

> *(She strikes it. First, nothing. She tries again – sparks! She starts a little fire.)*

Beware the ivory funnel mushroom

Be patient for the trout in the stream...

Trout!

*(A trout swims by. **WOODNUT** careful dips her hands in the water and gently tickles it...)*

Tickle, tickle, tickle...

(She whips out the trout, but it flips everywhere, jumps back in the stream. The trout makes a 'spolsh!'.)

Fine! Wasn't hungry away!

(The trout swims away.)

(She stares into the fire.)

Basterd sheriff. You ain't takin my dad too. I won't let ya.

(She goes through the bag and finds a pot of something.)

I know you said this would only work once, mum, if ever things got proper bad...

BALLADEER. This enchanted spot

All shimmer and hush

Where time has no place

A place between places

A place of great ancientness

Where the skin between worlds is thin

Where she came to drink Nature in...

*(As the song is sung, **WOODNUT** throws a pinch of powder into the fire. The flames smoke green. She daubs a thumb print of ash between her eyes. She looks about the forest. Over the fire, she stands, closes her eyes and casts a spell.)*

WOODNUT. Kind Spirits of the Great, Wild Wood!

Hear me!

I am not afraid!

I am not afraid to call upon thee!

Here my call, I beg you, and help me!

> (**WOODNUT** *opens her eyes and screams. Before her are a pair of 'wood spirits'. They are all skulls and skins and twigs and faces of twisted bark.*)

Bloody hell! It bloody worked!

> (*To the* **SPIRITS**.)

I thank you, kind spirits, for hearing my call.

> (*SSSHHHINGG! They both draw big knives.*)

SPIRIT 2. Be gone, child! This is no place for you!

SPIRIT 1. Run back the way you came, girl! While you still can!

> (*They lurch towards her. She almost runs –*)

WOODNUT. But I need your help. My father couldn't pay the king's tax and he went for the sheriff and now he's to hang!

SPIRIT 2. Rescuing menfolk is not our business. Go on, now.

WOODNUT. But if you won't help, then why did you come, good faeries?

SPIRIT 1. We're not faeries.

> (**SPIRIT 1** *remove their mask. This is* **MARY TUCK**.)

SPIRIT 2. What you doing? Don't take yer face off!

MARY. You're scaring no one, least of all her.

*(**SPIRIT 2** removes their mask. This is **JOAN LITTLE**, aka **LITTLE JOAN**.)*

WOODNUT. What are you?

MARY. We're just people, dear. I'm Mary Tuck. This is –

JOAN. Ah! Ah! No!

MARY. Just tell her your stage name then, Joan!

JOAN. *(Gives up.)* I'm Little Joan. I'm Joan Little. I'm… Joan.

WOODNUT. I'm Woodnut. I'm confused. Are you faeries?

MARY. We're outlaws, child. Hounded by the authorities.

JOAN. So we hide ourselves here, we blend in, we disappear!

WOODNUT. I thought the forest outlaws were wild, drooling beasts?

MARY. O, we have our moments.

JOAN. Tell me about it.

MARY. What's that supposed to mean?

JOAN. When you've had a few, you drool.

WOODNUT. No. You are woodland spirits! You're tricking me! I know it. Right, mum?

*(**WOODNUT** goes to her mother's grave and talks to her as:)*

MARY. Well, here's a sign from the solstice if ever I saw one. We hafto help her.

JOAN. Is your brain still drenched in last night's cyder? Help her how?

MARY. Her father's about to swing, Joan.

JOAN. *(To* **WOODNUT**.*)* Where's yer mother, child? Can't she take care of you?

WOODNUT. She's dead, kind wood spirit. Killed last week by a flaming arrow through the heart. *Ffftt!*

JOAN. Who by?

WOODNUT. Who else but the sheriff's men? And here she lies...your favourite spot, wannit mum?

MARY. Poor sapling! She deserves help. She called for us and we came. Brave thing.

*(***JOAN*** pulls ***MARY*** aside.)*

JOAN. We are in hiding, Mary. Wanted for treason. If we get caught in the world beyond this wood, we'll get hanged ourselves.

MARY. But we haven't left this forest in a year!

WOODNUT. *(To grave.)* Yes, mum. Wood spirits. Two of 'em. Your spell summoned 'em.

MARY. God love Nature's Mighty Works, but I swear, if I hafto eat another raw f'kin thrush egg...!

JOAN. I thought you were happy! I love our life. You talk to the trees. I perform to them. They're a perfect audience. We've put down roots here. We're happy, aren't we?

MARY. We can't hide forever. This is the call to arms we've been waiting for. Great! That's settled then!

WOODNUT. *(Stamps the fire out.)* Come, kind faeries! We gotta get to the hanging post! We can't be late!

*(***WOODNUT*** exits.)*

MARY. Come on, Joan. Let's live a little. And give the sheriff a show he won't forget!

*(***MARY*** chases after ***WOODNUT**.)*

JOAN. A show? Without rehearsal? Mary, wait! Bloody hell! Tell her we're not bloody faeries!

> *(Castle.)*

> *(Atop, the **KING** sits on his throne and sips his tea. Below in –)*

> *(The Grand Hall.)*

> *(The **BARONS BRASSWILT**, **BONEWEATHER** and **BRICKBROKE** enter.)*

BALLADEER. Who owns England? Who owns England?

Who owns the land where the hovel you live in sits on?

How did they acquire?

How did they conspire to own the lion's share of the dirt we walk on?

O, I'm sure it was regal

But was it really quite legal?

Bought and sold off with Nature's permission?

But here's another question...

If no one first owned this land, who did they buy it from?

If no one first owned this land, who did they buy it from?

Could it be they just took it?

Now that wouldn't be right...would it?

> *(**BALDWYN** enters.)*

BALDWYN. Baron Brasswilt, Baron Boneweather, Baron Brickbroke. The king's peace be with you.

BARONS. And with you.

BALDWYN. And who is this? Lurking in the gloom?

*(A fifth figure turns. This is **GISBURNE**, a puritanical mercenary for hire.)*

(Taken aback.) Gisburne! I don't remember inviting you into the council of barons –

BRASSWILT. Sir Gisburne is here at my expense, Baldwyn. Here to provide some added spine, if required.

BALDWYN. I'm sure we won't be needing any but...he is most welcome.

BONEWEATHER. Shall we to business?

BRASSWILT. The road?

BARONS. The road.

BALDWYN. The road! Of course! The gathering of taxes to pay for its construction went well and work continues apace –

BRICKBROKE. Then where is it?

BRASSWILT. We want our new estates signed over. There is hunting to be done. Follies to build.

BALDWYN. It is all in hand, my lords.

BRICKBROKE. Then why is it taking so damned long?

BALDWYN. Dissent in the village needed to be dealt with. This was swiftly quashed. Public protest is now outlawed. These new laws do not fall from the trees. I have to get them sanctioned by the king himself. This takes time. Effort. Gentle coercion.

*(During this, the **KING** sleepwalks from his throne and mumbles incoherently. **BALDWYN** deftly turns him around and sets him back.)*

BRICKBROKE. This is what we pay you for, Baldwyn. Yet not a single tree has been felled.

BARONS. What's going on?

BALDWYN. It...appears there is a small but cunning contingent deep at work in the forest. When my men attempt to clear the way, they are set upon.

BRASSWILT. By whom?

BALDWYN. That's the trouble. No one is ever seen. But the men who return are human pincushions. Pricked. Full of arrows.

BARONS. Outlaws.

BONEWEATHER. The solution is simple. Hunt them down and vanquish them.

BALDWYN. Easier said than done. They are tricky to track. Quick as smoke. Leave no trace.

GISBURNE. Then send me in.

(The air chills. **BALDWYN** *is silent.)*

BRASSWILT. What about it, Baldwyn? If your men cannot root out these troublemakers, Gisburne will.

BALDWYN. With respect, I am sheriff. The forest is my jurisdiction.

BONEWEATHER. The forest belongs to us. Or least it will, as soon as you do your job.

BRICKBROKE. You still want your job, don't you? Because we could easily promote Gisburne here –

BALDWYN. My lords, you know there is no man more suited for the position of sheriff than –

(Suddenly, **MARIAN** *crashes in through the main doors. She has a big goblet of something and seems half-cut.)*

MARIAN. I want to see him! Get off, Simpkins!

(She pushes off **SIMPKINS** *who's attempted to bar her from entering.)*

SIMPKINS. Sorry sir, tried to stop her –!

MARIAN. Husband? You're in a meeting! Surprise, surprise. How goes it, gents? Pfft! The smell of men together! Let's open a window in here eh? It is *musky!*

BONEWEATHER. Baldwyn, the grand hall is no place for wives.

BALDWYN. Marian, I am at work.

MARIAN. Simpkins gets more of your time than I do…

BALDWYN. *(Takes her into a corner.)* Have you been drinking again?

MARIAN. You promised me a forest hunt! You promised me blood!

BALDWYN. There are some executions later. Three commoners, about to be hanged.

MARIAN. I suppose that's something to look forward to.

BALDWYN. Go to the Hanging Post, grab yourself the best seat and I'll join you as soon as –

MARIAN. I'll wait here.

BALDWYN. Marian –

MARIAN. *I'll wait here.* And while I wait, I shall sew. Quietly.

(She whips out some needlework and sets her blurry-eyed attention to that whilst he returns to the **BARONS**.*)*

BALDWYN. Fear not. My wife is preoccupied and not one for politics.

MARIAN. Ow! (shit)

(She sucks her finger noisily.)

BALDWYN. My lords, there is no need for Gisburne's methods. I am the sheriff. Appointed by the king.

BRASSWILT. Paid for by us.

BRICKBROKE. His methods are effective.

BALDWYN. No man is above the law.

GISBURNE. That depends on whose laws you abide by.

BALDWYN. I will personally man an elite squad to eradicate these entrenched ne'er-do-wells! Once caught, we will begin the decimation of the forest and the redistribution of the land it sits on...

> (**SIMPKINS** *pulls down a map of the forest. It is divided into three estates, with a baron's name on each section. The* **BARONS** *study it approvingly.*)

Do not forget, my public executions go a long way towards reminding the people of what happens if they dare rise above their stations again. Speaking of which! I must put in an appearance at the Hanging Post... my dear...?

> (*But* **MARIAN** *is fast asleep, snoring slightly, embroidery still in one hand, goblet just about to spill in the other.* **BALDWYN** *saves the cup.*)

I shall leave you to sleep it off, sweet Marian...

> (*He covers her with a blanket.*)

Come, my lords! To the Hanging Post!

> (*They all exit.* **GISBURNE** *is the last to leave. He gives* **MARIAN** *a strange look before exiting.*)

(The Hanging Post – a place of torture and execution set at the foot of the King's Castle.)

(The **BALLADEER** *gives us a tour of the tortures as the nooses rise up.* **BALDWYN** *proudly oversees, with* **SIMPKINS** *beside him.)*

BALLADEER. It's a stroke of genius on Baldwyn's part

To make public all punishments

Up here on the blood-drenched meat deck

There's round-the-clock tortures in painfully plain sight

Up here, you're skinned for your sins

Lawbreakers! Transgressors! Plus, the hungry,

The homeless, the old, the crippled, the young,

And all you in between, desperate to live,

You'll be up here quick as a flash and lashed

For trespassing in the King's forest... I mean, honestly!

Those caught stealing his apples, his 'firewood'

Or hunting his deer, face the first of three warnings:

Caught once, you get your two vital bow fingers *chopped!*

(A **TORTURER** *brings down a hatchet. CHOP!!! "ARRRGHHH!!!" Digits fly.* **BALDWYN** *picks up a* **SEVERED FINGER** *and studies it.)*

BALDWYN. No more archery for you...

BALLADEER. Caught twice, you're blinded by white-hot irons –

*(A **TORTURER** sinks white-hot pokers in – "AAAAHHHH!" Eyeless, grotesque.)*

BALDWYN. Starting to get the message, are we?

BALLADEER. Caught stealing a third time, they stick yer neck in a noose and – *CRRRICKKK!!!!*

*(Three folks are shoved into position before each noose by an executioner. One is **BOB MUCH**, one is a young glove-wearing lockpick, **WILLIAM SCATLOCKE**, and the third is **BETTY**, the old woman from the village.)*

Hang ya 'til yer dead!

Now there's those who've disobeyed so great

That they graduate straight to the hangman's rope

Like these three here. A rescue? Really? Well, we can hope.

*(**BALDWYN** steps onto the platform.)*

BALDWYN. Three criminals today defied the King's Law. Let their deaths be a reminder to you all!

*(Reads a parchment, to **BOB**.)*

For the avoidance of payment of the King's tax and attempting to skewer an officer of the crown – you are to be hanged b'the neck. Do you have anything to say?

BOB. Just get it done. The sooner I can join my beloved wife, the better.

BALDWYN. The King's Peace Be With You.

(A noose goes over his head.)

*(To **WILL**.)* For the avoidance of payment of the King's tax and breaking and entering into Baron

Boneweather's summer folly, stealing a barrel of salt herring, two patterned rugs, one silver spoon and a beloved portrait of his grandmother Florence...you are to be hanged b'the neck. Do you have anything to say?

WILL. Only this:

(To **CROWD.***)*

Pickin locks is the easy bit, kids. It's the carrying off what takes the skill.

BALDWYN. The King's Peace Be With You.

(A noose goes over **WILL***'s head.)*

(To **BETTY.***)* For avoidance of payment of the King's tax, for resisting arrest and breaking the noses of several of the sheriff's men, you are to be hanged b'the –

*(***SIMPKINS** *hands him a note.)*

It seems your debt has been paid by a mysterious benefactor and you may go free.

*(***BETTY** *is taken out of the noose.)*

BETTY. I'd prefer to hang, thanks all the same.

SIMPKINS. You're free, old woman! Go home!

BETTY. *(As she's dragged away)* You'll be sorry you didn't hang me! I'll be back for you all! Never relax, sheriff!

(At the back of the **CROWD***,* **WOODNUT** *arrives with a panting* **MARY** *and* **JOAN** *behind her. They're in 'disguise' with their masks on.)*

WOODNUT. There's my dad! His head's in the noose! What's the plan?

*(***MARY** *and* **JOAN** *are silent.* **MARY** *looks at* **JOAN.***)*

MARY. Over to you Joan.

JOAN. Me? What can I do?

MARY. Distract 'em with a speech, a skit, a crude nautical sonnet?

JOAN. I haven't played a crowd this big for years. *(Suddenly terrified.)* I can't go on.

WOODNUT. What's happening?

MARY. She's got stage fright.

> *(Back to the platform.)*

BALDWYN. And now, to punish the guilty...

> *(**SIMPKINS** goes to push **BOB** from the trap into thin air. One... Two... Thr –)*

WOODNUT. Wait!

> *(She runs to the stage. The **VILLAGERS** gasp.)*

This man is my father and he's done nothing wrong!

BALDWYN. You again?

BOB. Woodnut, what are you doing?

WOODNUT. It's a rescue, dad! Don't panic! Everything's under con –

> *(**SIMPKINS** grabs **WOODNUT**.)*

WOODNUT. *(Struggling to speak.)* This man's my dad! And my mother – Jenny Much! She stood against the – geddoff!

BOB. Let her go!

WOODNUT. She fought for the forest cus the barons wanna cut a road right through it and –

BALDWYN. Silence her, Simpkins!

(**WOODNUT** *bites* **SIMPKINS**' *hand.*)

SIMPKINS. Ow!

WOODNUT. MY MOTHER WAS KILLED BY THE SHERIFF AND I SHALL HAVE MY REVENGE!

BALDWYN. (*To the* **CROWD**, *pointing to* **BOB**.) It was this man's wife who whipped up dissent which led to my men breaking their sticks across your backs. Don't let such ideas fester again. Next time, I shan't be so lenient. Now, hang this scum!

BOB. Woodnut, don't look!

BALDWYN. No! Be sure to watch, girl. Your father couldn't teach you obedience, but I will.

WOODNUT. Kind Spirits of the Wild Wood! Help us!

> (**SIMPKINS** *goes to hang them when – FEEEE-SHHTTTT!!!! – an arrow lands right before her feet. She jumps back.*)

SIMPKIN. Bloody hell!

BALDWYN. Who did that?

> (*Everyone looks up to where the arrow came from and spots a* **HOODED FIGURE** *stood high up on the battlements, their long-bow string taut with a second arrow primed. Everyone points and whispers.*)

(*To the* **HOODED FIGURE**.) Whoever you are...you should know, to delay an execution is a criminal offence. Simpkins? Continue.

> (**SIMPKINS** *dithers.*)

It's just a little arrow! Stop dithering and hang them!

> (**SIMPKINS** *is both terrified and mesmerised by the* **HOODED FIGURE**.)

Very well. I shall do it myself.

>   (**BALDWYN** *goes to push them off but – FFFF-CHONNNNGGG!!!! – gets an arrow through the boot, pinning him to the floor. He screams.*)

SIMPKINS. Sir! O God! Are you alright, sir?

BALDWYN. *(To* **HOOD.***)* If you hadn't broken the law already, friend, you've certainly broken it now! Guards!

>   (*FFFSSTT!!! This one, in the other boot. He screams.*)

That's definitely broken the skin!

SIMPKINS. What should I do, sir?

WOODNUT. Best let us go, sheriff. That next arrow won't land between yer toes...

BALDWYN. Simpkins! Release them!

>   (**SIMPKINS** *de-nooses* **BOB** *and* **WILL.***)*

WILL. What? Me as well? Sweet!

WOODNUT. *(To* **HOOD.***)* Thank you, kind spirit.

>   (**HOOD** *nods. Suddenly,* **GISBURNE** *steps out of nowhere and fires his crossbow – BBBTTT!!!!* **HOOD** *turns at the last second, but it grazes their arm.* **GISBURNE** *takes aim again but* **WOODNUT** *stands in* **GISBURNE***'s way. He throws her aside.* **WOODNUT**, **BOB** *and* **WILL** *dash through the* **CROWD**. **GISBURNE** *scans the battlements where* **HOOD** *just stood.*)

GISBURNE. *(To* **MEN.***)* I clipped him! Look for a man with a wounded arm!

MEN. Yes, Sir Gisburne!

WOODNUT, WILL & VILLAGERS. *(Whisper into roar.)* Who was that?

Who was he?

Who was that hooded –?

Did you see what he –?

Where'd he go?

Quick as smoke!

He dares to take a –

He's there, then he's gone!

This hooded one –

Such lethal aim!

Like a shadow –

The skill!

The cheek!

The Hood!

He's Hood!

Hood! *Hood!* HOOD!

BALDWYN. Shut up! Shut up shut up SHUT UP! Go home!

>   *(To* **SIMPKINS.***)*

Scour the kingdom! Find me that hooded man!

SIMPKINS. *(To the* **GUARDS.***)* Find the hooded man!!!

SHERIFF'S MEN. Find the hooded man!

>   *(The* **SHERIFF'S MEN** *run in all directions and disperse out into the kingdom.* **ROBIN HOOD** *bounds in again.)*

ROBIN HOOD. Huzzah! The chase is on! The sheriff's men come for me!

BALLADEER. They're not after you. They're after somebody else.

ROBIN HOOD. I distinctly heard my old nemesis the sheriff say –

BALLADEER. 'Hooded Man'. Is what he said.

ROBIN HOOD. Which is me. Isn't it?

BALLADEER. Took an arrow to the arm, did you?

ROBIN HOOD. But I remember doing something like this... once upon a time.

BALLADEER. This isn't some fairy tale. We're telling the true story. What actually happened.

ROBIN HOOD. Aren't I what actually happened?

*(**BALLADEER** shakes her head regretfully. **ROBIN HOOD**'s tiny mind is blown.)*

Right. Hm. I feel a bit funny...

*(The **BALLADEER** gently escorts him off.)*

(Castle.)

*(**GISBURNE** bursts into the grand chamber. **MARIAN**, blanket still about her, wakes with a groggy jolt.)*

MARIAN. Don't you knock?

GISBURNE. I'm looking for a man. In a hood. Have you seen him?

MARIAN. A man? In a hood? Alright Gisburne, I confess, I have him stuffed here under my blanket, but he's made me swear not to tell anyone. Especially you. Where's my husband? Have I missed the hangings? Would you like a drink?

(**GISBURNE** *has no time for this nonsense and exits. When* **MARIAN** *knows she's alone, she exhales, drops the act and allows her face to crumple with pain. She pulls away the blanket to reveal a nasty wound in her upper arm – a graze from a crossbow bolt.* **MARIAN** *pours her drink on to her wound to clean it. She grabs her needlepoint and sews up her wound.)*

That went well.

(Forest. Underground...beneath the trees, a network of roots.)

(The gang arrive, breathless.)

WOODNUT. Did we lose 'em?

JOAN. They won't find us down here.

WOODNUT. What is this place?

MARY. The Underground Forest. Our secret sanctuary amongst the roots and worms.

JOAN. We'll lay low 'til we're sure they're gone. Sorry Woodnut. I froze at the worst moment.

MARY. I thought you lived for timing! Lucky we were saved by that dashing, devilish –

WOODNUT. Hood.

WILL. He was incredible! Part of your gang, is he?

JOAN. Uhh, I'm sorry. Who the hell are you?

WILL. O. Will Scatlocke. Lock picker. Heart breaker. Lovable rogue.

JOAN. You can't just follow us into our secret hide-out. We don't know you.

BOB. *(To* **MARY** *and* **JOAN.***)* We don't know you, either. Woodnut, who are these people?

WOODNUT. Mary Tuck and Little Joan. That's all I know.

JOAN. Good. Because our pasts must remain a complete –

MARY. I was a sister at St Agnes abbey. I prayed furiously for a shred of grace but could not stop the boiling rage I felt for the bishops who bloated themselves on honey ale and roast deer. They caught me pissing in the beer barrels. I was brought before Baldwyn and forced to apologise… It did not end well. As for Joan here, she was the King's clown. A real class act back in the day –

JOAN. Alright, I'll tell my life story, thank you. I was the King's clown…well, apprentice fool at his court, to be specific. But he bloody loved me. I was his favourite. He'd get me to tell him little fairy tales. I'd play tricks on him, teach him silly dances…

*(***KING*** appears in memory.)*

KING. O Joany, you are a smasher…

(The **KING** *fades.)*

JOAN. He was a sweet man back then. Then the sheriff took over and took a keen dislike to me. I refused to budge… It did not end well.

*(***MARY*** hands out drinks to everyone.)*

MARY. The noose beckoned for us both.

JOAN. So we fled for our lives.

MARY. Ran deep into these woods.

JOAN. And here we collided. A disgraced nun who's embraced Mother Nature –

MARY. And an exiled court fool with stage fright, both with a shared hatred of Baldwyn.

WILL. I hate Baldwyn.

BOB. I hate Baldwyn.

WOODNUT. We all hate Baldwyn.

MARY. There we are. Once we were strangers, now we have a common cause. Drink up!

(Castle. Grand Chamber.)

*(***MARIAN*** paces as ***BALDWYN*** has the arrow removed from his boot by ***SIMPKINS****.)*

BALDWYN. Ow! Raid the villages! Ransack the ah! – houses! Find out who this Hood is and bring him to me! Oof!

MARIAN. It's just a scratch.

BALDWYN. Ruined my boots. These were Italian! I'll chop off his bow-fingers myself!

SIMPKINS. He's obviously a cracking shot, sir. That's who we should be hunting down. Crack-shots.

MARIAN. Good idea, Simpkins. Force every soul in the kingdom to try and shoot an arrow between your toes, husband, and the one that does, must be him!

BALDWYN. The miller and his brat escaped. They must be in league with this Hood. And where did Gisburne spring from?! Pirouetting for the barons while I was pinned to the floor! I've got to rid the forest of outlaws once and for all!

MARIAN. Husband! Calm yourself. You need permission from the king. You need to heal. You couldn't ride into the forest for at least what…?

SIMPKINS. Three days, sir.

BALDWYN. Then in three days, we ride! I cannot lose the trust of the barons –

MARIAN. Or their lucrative backhanders!

BALDWYN. These outlaws must be exterminated. The road must go ahead. And Hood must hang!

>*(Forest. Next morning.)*

>*(**MARIAN** enters. She is hooded. She looks about the glade. She listens. Stillness. Silence. Too silent.)*

BALLADEER. Tread careful now

Keep your provenance disguised

These woods have new protectors now

And this forest, many eyes...

MARIAN. Hello?

>*(**MARIAN** takes a step forward and is suddenly ensnared in a trap set by **JOAN** and **MARY**, masked.)*

WOODNUT. Got 'em!

>*(**MARIAN** is tackled by **WILL** and **BOB** who wear their own slightly less impressive line in facial forest freakery. **WILL** gets carried away.)*

WILL. What we got here, eh? Looks like a wanderer's lost their way in the woods! Smells like a wealthy one! Wafts of Egyptian lavender!

MARIAN. Unhand me!

WILL. Not 'til you cough up yer cash!

>*(He pulls a knife but **MARY** grabs him by the wrist.)*

MARY. Ah, ah! We only use knives for show.

WILL. Eh?

*(Suddenly **WILL** gets a fist to the jaw and falls back. **MARIAN**, gets to her feet.)*

MARIAN. *(Furious, shaken.)* For god's sakes! What is this? I came to help but perhaps I shouldn't have bothered!

*(She throws off the ropes but has her hood up, so as not to be recognised. Everyone sees her and goes slack-jawed. They point in awe. **MARIAN** doesn't notice at first.)*

Sheriff Baldwyn will be coming through here in three days and –

(She sees them all looking.)

What?

WOODNUT. You're Hood! From yesterday!

MARIAN. O. Yes.

WILL. Sir. My lord. Lord Sir Hood, I think you're brilliant.

WOODNUT. We've been talking about you all night –

WILL. Are you looking for a sidekick to carry your stuff? Because I am available.

WOODNUT. Who are you under there, wood spirit?

WILL. Show us. Let us see the face of the man to who we all owe our very lives.

MARIAN. I would rather not.

BOB. Well, not trusting anyone, we'd rather you did.

*(**BOB** pulls back the hood to reveal her face.)*

MARIAN. I wear the hood for a reason!

BOB. I can see why now.

WILL. Eh?! What's going on?! I don't understand...

MARY. What is your name?

MARIAN. I must remain a mystery, for your sake as well as my own.

BOB. "Mystery?" Who does she think she is?

WOODNUT. Dad! Shh! She saved your life.

BOB. I didn't ask her to.

MARIAN. Look, I only came to let you know the sheriff's on the rampage. I know you two lurk about these parts.

JOAN. You've seen us?

MARIAN. You're pretty easy to spot with all your soliloquys to the trees.

JOAN. You didn't spot us a moment ago.

MARIAN. Three days from now, hide. In your secret underground wotsit.

>   (**MARY** and **JOAN** look at each other. **MARIAN** makes to leave.)

WILL. Hold hard. Let's not forget…the whiff of Egyptian lavender!

JOAN. Why help us? What's in it for you?

MARIAN. If anything, I wish for a clean conscience.

BOB. O, piss off.

WOODNUT. Dad!

BOB. Daughter, she's rich. She's one of them.

WOODNUT. She shot the rotten sheriff right through his boots!

>   (*To* **MARIAN**.) Why don't you join us?

ALL. What?

WILL. Woah, there! She can't join. She's not Hood. She can't be.

WOODNUT. Let her fire an arrow...through this apple! Then you'll see –

(**WOODNUT** *plucks an apple and balances it on her head.*)

BOB. O no ya don't.

(*As* **BOB** *takes it off her head – FFTT!!! – in his hands, an apple with an arrow through it.*)

Bloody hell!

WOODNUT. (*In awe.*) She's Hood alright. It's meant to be that we ran into you. You should've heard the villagers yesterday. As we ran through, they were like *Who was that? Who was Hood?* You're a thing! You should be Hood, full time. We could help.

MARIAN. I'm sorry. I can't.

WOODNUT. But it's happening already. Think of the good Hood could do.

MARIAN. I prefer to help you from afar.

WILL. Are you afraid?

MARIAN. I'm not afraid. I risk my life even talking to you.

WOODNUT. She took an arrow to the arm saving us. I saw it happen!

WILL. If you don't wanna do it that's fine. I can be Hood.

MARIAN. What?

WILL. I'd do a voice and everything. Which you can't. O, yeh. A few threatening words and *bosh!* They'll be fillin' their britches when they see me.

MARIAN. You can't just stick a sack over your head and beat up some barons. That was never the intention. Besides, Hood is my thing. And works best silent.

WOODNUT. Will's right though. Hood does scare them.

BOB. Does he?

WOODNUT. To them, he's a shadow. A will o' the wisp. A ghost from the haunted woods.

JOAN. *(Examining hood.)* It's a strong look. Potentially quite iconic as disguises go.

MARIAN. I mean, it was the first thing I grabbed when I left the house. Just a random idea of mine.

WILL. Puh.

MARIAN. What is your problem? Don't you trust me?

WILL. Not as far as I could chuck ya, lady.

>   (**MARY** *wails as if the trees are talking to her. This shuts everyone up. Seized by the spirit of the wood, she starts to incant.*)

>   (**JOAN** *takes the hood from* **MARIAN** *and gives it to* **MARY**.)

MARY. If ideas are seeds, then stories are trees

Let us whisper this myth on the far-ranging breeze

Held in the branches of the Great Wild Wood

We are one, we are all, we are one, we are Hood!

ALL. We Are Hood.

JOAN. Are we sure about this?

MARY. Bit late now. I've incanted the oath. The band is forged!

WOODNUT. Let's put this Hood to the test!

>   *(An old path through the forest.)*

>   (*The* **BARONS BONEWEATHER, BRICKBONE** *and* **BRASSWILT** *trot down the road. The forest [the gang] creep up behind them.*

There's a sound and their horses bolt. They crash to the ground. Ahead of him, stands **HOOD**, *face hidden.)*

BONEWEATHER. Who are you? What do you want?

(When **HOOD** *speaks, it's other-worldly and unnerves the* **BARONS**.*)*

HOOD. I am Hood. Money.

BARONS. What money?

(Suddenly, that **HOOD** *vanishes and another* **HOOD** *appears elsewhere.)*

HOOD. The money you took from the village.

BRICKBROKE. Taxes lawfully collected –

BRASSWILT. Authorised by the King himself.

BONEWEATHER. This is robbery. You are trespassing.

HOOD. *(Another one, another spot.)* Hand it over!

BARONS. This land belongs to us now.

(The forest sighs. The **BARONS** *look about. The air is tinged with something strange...)*

HOOD. *(Another.)* Do you hear that? The forest whispers...

(Another.) "You do not own me...and you never will..."

(Suddenly – FFFTT!!! FFT!!! FFT-WANGG!!! An arrow nicks each of their cheeks.)

BARONS. Ahh! Buh!! GAHH!!!

HOOD. *(Another.) Money.*

(They throw purses at the various **HOODS**.*)*

BARONS. Here! Take my purse! Not the face! Don't kill us!

HOOD. *(Another.)* Feels good, doesn't it, to give a something back...?

> *(**MARIAN** fires and three arrows embed into the buttock of each Baron. They yelp and scarper.)*

> *(The **BARONS** flee in terror. **JOAN**, **MARY**, **WILL** and **WOODNUT** emerge.)*

JOAN. Well, that was great!

MARIAN. I think I'm going to like this.

BOB. We're rich!

> *(**MARIAN** tosses the bag of gold to **WOODNUT**.)*

WOODNUT. I'm taking this money back to the village!

WILL. What?!

(Village.)

> *(**WOODNUT** runs through the village, handing back coins to everyone. The **VILLAGERS** are thrilled.)*

WOODNUT. From Hood... From Hood...courtesy of Hood, Betty...

BETTY. That's very kind of him!

> *(**WOODNUT** exits. **SIMPKINS** enters. She feels Betty's joy and frowns.)*

SIMPKINS. What are you so happy about?

*(To **BETTY**, on the quiet.)* I've brought you some scraps from the castle. Don't eat 'em all at once.

BETTY. I don't need yer scraps anymore, Sandra. I've money enough for food this week. And fuel. And hell's teeth, I might even get that hole in the roof fixed!

SIMPKINS. Where are you getting money from? Mum? Mum?

BETTY. That nice Mr Hood's given it to us.

SIMPKINS. *What?!*

> *(Castle.* **KING***'s chambers.)*

> *(***BALDWYN** *pours a cup of tea for the* **KING** *and waits for him to drink from it. He then offers the* **KING** *papers. The* **KING** *looks at them confused.)*

BALDWYN. We're clearing the forest of outlaws, your majesty. I require your immediate authorisation. Here, here and here...

KING. *(Drifts off.)* I'm very fond of that forest. I used to play there as a child, with my eight sisters. "Thistle, Thistle, Blossom, Whistle" and "Buffets!" Ever played a game of Buffets, Anthony?

BALDWYN. *(Tries to get him to sign.)* Can't say I have, your majesty.

KING. A vicious game! I've still got dog-jaw from it.

BALDWYN. "Dog-jaw" your majesty?

KING. Yes. It's quite a thing. Here, feel this...

> *(The* **KING** *strokes the side of his jaw and leans over to let* **BALDWYN** *touch his jaw too. When* **BALDWYN** *does, the* **KING** *barks at him.* **BALDWYN** *jumps.)*

Got ya there, didn't I Anthony? The old "dog-jaw" gag.

BALDWYN. Certainly did, sir. Very good, sir.

> *(The* **KING** *signs.)*

Thank you, sir.

*(Exasperated, **BALDWYN** exits with the papers.)*

KING. Come back soon, Anthony! It's nice to have the company. Bring your charming lady wife. Or even Simpkins! Anybody, really...

*(**BALDWYN**'s quarters.)*

(He enters and exhales slowly, trying to get a grip. Nearby is a small chest with a lock on it.)

BALDWYN. Simpkins, we have the all-clear to proceed. The old fool signed eventually but remind me to up his dose. Simpkins? Where is she?

CREEPY SQUEAKY VOICES. She's not here...

It's just us...

*(**BALDWYN** looks to the chest.)*

BALDWYN. Not now, my pretty ones... Daddy's at work...

CREEPY SQUEAKY VOICES. But we miss you...

we have something to tell you...

Release usss...*releasssse*...

BALDWYN. I'll hafto be quick.

*(Looking around, he unlocks a chest. The 'voices' are released, and **BALDWYN** lights up when he sees them, but we don't. Not yet.)*

CREEPY SQUEAKY VOICES. Keep her close...she wanders... she roams...

BALDWYN. Who? Simpkins?

CREEPY SQUEAKY VOICES. No, ya big ninny! *Her!*

(*Enter* **MARIAN**, *looking tousled and exhausted, but alive.* **BALDWYN** *slams the chest closed, locks and covers it.*)

MARIAN. What is it with that damnable chest? What do you keep in there? A secret lover?

BALDWYN. Not at all, my dear. You know it's simply my private business. Work-related. Hush hush.

MARIAN. When do you clean up the forest?

BALDWYN. Tomorrow. I shall flush out the outlaws. I'm calling it *The Purge*. What do you think?

MARIAN. Suitably chilling.

BALDWYN. It's not meant to be chilling. I'm not that lunatic Gisburne. I don't want to kill *everyone*. After all, people can't pay tax when they're dead!

MARIAN. The poor barons would be destitute!

BALDWYN. As would we, my love. For the sake of our future why don't you join me?

(**MARIAN** *is silent.*)

You love to ride. You're always off to the forest. And you're quite good with a bow. We could spend the day together.

MARIAN. I don't wish to spend it slaying outlaws. I'm tired. Tired now. Tired tomorrow.

BALDWYN. Either way, I want you close.

MARIAN. Why do I feel like you're suspecting me of something?

BALDWYN. I just want to give you some attention, that's all. I've been so busy and you've grown listless…

(**MARIAN** *suddenly tries to open the chest.* **BALDWYN** *stops her. It's playful. Sort of. He plucks a leaf from her hair.*)

I remember when we both had leaves in our hair. Back in the early days when we'd spend hours galloping through the woods together. You remember, don't you?

MARIAN. Yes. I remember.

(*Enter the* **BARONS** *and* **SIMPKINS** *with a crash. They all burst in talking over each other, grabbing* **BALDWYN**, *trying to explain:* "Hood!", "It's Hood!", "We saw him!", *etc.*)

BALDWYN. What? Hood? Where?

BARONS/SIMPKINS. In the depths of the forest! / Right there, in the village! / Bold as brass!

And he robbed me! Stole my hard-earned gold! / He's giving it to the poor!

BONEWEATHER. The man is a menace!

BRASSWILT. He has a strange sorcery!

BRICKBROKE. The forest was his ally!

BALDWYN. What the devil do you mean?

BRASSWILT. I mean he was here! He was there! He was every-bloody-where!

BONEWEATHER. This situation is getting out of hand. It's time to let Gisburne off the leash!

MARIAN. No!

(*Beat.*)

No to Gisburne because...my brilliant husband is trying his hardest and he is the Law and he was just telling me about his cunning plan to catch Hood.

BONEWEATHER. Was he?

MARIAN. He was! And it's completely ingenious. *An archery contest!* Open to all, but one that is a trap cleverly disguised. It will surely lure Hood out of hiding because he's a cocky swine in love with his own reflection and he won't be able to resist showing off his skills. When he does, we will have him! It will be tomorrow. Hood will be dead by dusk. Problem solved.

BONEWEATHER. An excellent plan, Baldwyn. But you hang by a thread. See that this devil is done with.

*(The **BARONS** exit.)*

BALDWYN. But my love, the Purge is scheduled for tomorrow.

MARIAN. What's more important? Hood is surely the ringleader. Catch Hood and you sever the head of the dissenters.

BALDWYN. Do you really think he'll show?

MARIAN. If he's as arrogant as they say he is, I'd bet my life on it.

*(Fanfare. **SIMPKINS**, on the balcony.)*

SIMPKINS. Hear ye! Hear ye! The king has decreed in all of his benevolence to hold an archery contest, tomorrow, outside the castle walls! He who displays the greatest skill will be deemed greatest in the land and will win one hundred nobles!

*(The **VILLAGERS** all sit up when they hear that.)*

There will also be free beer!

(The kingdom cheers wildly.)

BALLADEER. From the wood comes acorn to oak

When Nature's drunk she embraces all folk

See the long bow in the branch of the yew

Within the sycamore tree arrows fly true

Wood for to cut and wood for to carve

To do or to die? To sup or to starve?

> *(Throughout the song, **WOODNUT** finds her bow, bends it and strings it. She finishes making her own arrows. She has a quiver of them now. She tries to shoot one as **MARIAN** walks by and dumps more purses of gold in a pile.)*

MARIAN. More money for the village.

> *(She eyes **WOODNUT**.)*

The contest is a trap you know. Designed to catch Hood.

> *(The **BALLADEER** watches.)*

WOODNUT. Could you teach me how to shoot?

MARIAN. I don't have the time.

WOODNUT. *(Squinting, trying to aim.)* I tell you who's out of time. The sheriff. His days are numbered.

MARIAN. You seek revenge for your mother?

WOODNUT. Of course. He killed her. If he hadn't ordered his men to –

> *(She tries to shoot but fails.)*

MARIAN. I'm sorry. I wish there was something I could do –

WOODNUT. You could be my new mother if you like?

MARIAN. Me? No. I cannot.

WOODNUT. Why not?

MARIAN. I have no interest.

WOODNUT. Don't you like me?

MARIAN. No. I mean, I do. I mean. You're fine. But I don't like children in general.

WOODNUT. God. Me neither.

MARIAN. I think they're vastly over-rated.

WOODNUT. Same. Same.

> *(She fails to fire an arrow again.)*

Dammit.

MARIAN. I'm sorry. I hafto go. Remember to stay underground. The sheriff's men are everywhere. So don't even think of going to that contest.

> *(**MARIAN** exits, walking by **WILL** going in the opposite direction.)*

WILL. Must be nice.

MARIAN. What's that?

WILL. To go back to your life of luxury whenever you get bored of all this.

> *(**MARIAN** watches him continue on his way. She exits.)*
>
> *(Elsewhere in the forest, **MARY** and **BOB** begin a spiritual journey.)*

MARY. *(To **BOB**, with cup.)* Drink this.

BOB. What is it?

MARY. It's a concoction to rid you of despair. Your broken spirit needs to be healed.

BOB. It smells funny.

MARY. It's Ivory Funnel. The sepulchre mushroom. I've no marshmallow to hide the bitter taste.

BOB. Ivory Funnel? Isn't that –?

MARY. Drink.

BOB. My wife was always trying to get me into this kind of thing... to lure me into the forest to find fairy rings... I was always too busy milling... if you could see me now, Jenny –

(He toasts and drinks.)

MARY. Good. Now, you must know that the Ivory Funnel can cause terrible confusions, nightmarish visions and agonising death –

BOB. *(Sudden panic post-swallow.) Now* you tell me?!

MARY. One drop brings befuddlement. Three drops turns everything tartan. Five drops allows you to connect with the world on a profound level. Never, ever take more than five. You'd tumble into the next realm and never come back.

BOB. How many have I had?

MARY. Just enough, pilgrim.

BOB. Not sure about this.

MARY. Too late, mate. Go with it. Breathe in...breathe out...now take yer shirt off.

*(Elsewhere, **WILL** and **JOAN** enter and drop more bags of money.)*

WILL. I tell ya Joan, there's something fishy about her. Who helps folk out for no reason? It's not right. Look, I'm happy the village are getting some coin back but it's all a bit goody-two-shoes, don't ya think?

JOAN. I've seen her somewhere before...

WILL. Have ya?

JOAN. She was just a face in the crowd. But she was there alright, in the king's court.

WILL. I wish she'd bloody stayed there.

JOAN. I liked it when it was just me and Mary. My nerves can't handle all this adventure. I'm not a coward, Will. I've played to thousands. But after the sheriff threw me out, all bloodied and beaten... He owes me.

WILL. He owes us our lives.

(**WILL** *pulls a glove off to reveal his two bow fingers missing.*)

Took my fingers off personally, he did. With his little knife. Now for a skilled lockpick and a picker of pockets you can imagine how damaging losing these vital digits is. I'll never be an outlaw of legend. Not unless I get that hood.

WILL. If I had the hood I'd be less pinchy, more punchy. None of this 'no violence' rubbish. To be remembered, you've got to make a dent.

JOAN. And who will remember Little Joan? No one. I guarantee it.

WILL. Where is she, by the way?

JOAN. Archery contest.

WILL. What? As Hood? Without us?

(*Elsewhere* **BOB** *is now tripping his face off and talking to a tree.*)

BOB. I can feel you...your roots, deep below...the nerves of the forest *sing*...the trees are breathing...talking...

MARY. *(Sat watching.)* Go on.

BOB. It's like...this tree just *is*. It's just living. Right now. It's serving its purpose. It exists. But it's not sad. It's not angry. It doesn't want to kill Baldwyn...kill Baldwyn... *KILL BALDWYN!*

> (**BOB** *descends into cosmic terror.*)

MARY. Let's go look at summin over here!

> (*A clearing.* **WOODNUT** *practices her archery still.* **WILL** *approaches.*)

WILL. You don't give up, I'll give ya that. Have you heard? There's an archery contest.

WOODNUT. She says it's a trap.

WILL. How does she know?

WOODNUT. She said it's got the sheriff's fingerprints all over it.

WILL. But there's a cash prize and free beer. You could compete. I could drink.

WOODNUT. She said it'll be dangerous and that we should hide.

WILL. Who's she to tell you what to do? She's not yer mother.

WOODNUT. No. She's not.

WILL. Besides, she's there.

WOODNUT. Is she?

WILL. Come on. We're outlaws. Outlaws don't do as they're told. They go against the grain. We'll go in disguise. No one will know it's us. Who knows, maybe we'll hit something.

WOODNUT. Yeh. Like the sheriff.

> (*Back with* **MARY** *and* **BOB** *...who's at the heart of his journey now.*)

MARY. How did she die...?

BOB. She was protecting the forest. She had asked to speak with the barons, to beg them to stop the road. They had invited us to the castle for negotiations. It was night. A blood-moon. A small group of us made our way to the castle. Jenny was at the front. Before the castle gates we saw 'em. An army of his men waiting for us. From out of the darkness, Baldwyn's men shot a flaming arrow into the air. It fell like a star. We watched it as it arced down t'ward us. Stood open-mouthed as it came closer...closer. It pierced Jenny straight through the heart.

> *(Suddenly, the **BALLADEER** is struck by an arrow through the heart. The forest screams. **BOB** catches her and carries her to the ground.)*

She died in my arms, right before my eyes. I buried her the next day. When Jenny died, the fight died with her.

BALLADEER/JENNY. No. The fight still lives.

> *(**BOB** resurfaces with a jolt from the dream-state but **JENNY** is still right before him.)*

JENNY. Bob, I'm here! Can you see me? Can you hear me? Look after her!

> *(But he can't hear her.)*

BOB. My Jenny...

MARY. Strong, aren't they? Those mushrooms...

> *(Castle.)*

> *(In the **KING**'s chambers, **BALDWYN** enters to find the **KING** talking to himself. Teapot and cup are set nearby. **SIMPKINS** comes in behind **BALDWYN** and stands in readiness.)*

KING. Once upon a time... Once upon a time...

BALDWYN. Everything alright, your majesty...?

KING. I'm trying to remember a story but my mind's a muddle...what comes next? Once upon a time...

BALDWYN. There was a handsome prince? A frog? A beast?

KING. There was a mighty king! Yes, that's the one! I am still king, aren't I Anthony?

BALDWYN. But of course you are, your majesty! Which is why, if you wouldn't mind just signing here, and here, and here...

KING. Yes, but first I should get dressed in my royal finery! Would you help me please, Simpkins?

(As **SIMPKINS** *swoops in,* **BALDWYN** *stops her.)*

BALDWYN. Remind me why you're getting dressed up in your royal finery, your majesty?

KING. Because we're holding an archery contest today and I thought it would be nice to reconnect with me people. Thank you, Simpkins.

*(***BALDWYN** *stops her.)*

BALDWYN. O, not really necessary your majesty. Besides, you can't stand sporting events...

KING. Really? When did I say that? I thought I loved archery.

BALDWYN. Your majesty, I must insist –

KING. Anthony, I know you're concerned, but I want to go and you cannot stop me. Because, as you so clearly pointed out a moment ago, I am still king. Thank you, Simpkins.

*(**SIMPKINS** dresses the **KING**.)*

Now –

*(Takes **BALDWYN**'s papers.)*

What's this for?

BALDWYN. It's a death warrant, your majesty, for a particularly disruptive character goes by the name of Hood.

KING. O! I've been hearing about this fellow. Proper slippery eel. Nobody knows who he is. It could be anyone, they say. Anyone of my subjects. It could be Simpkins, right Simpkins?

*(**SIMPKINS** mimes firing a little bow.)*

Hood could even be me, Anthony... ME.

*(**BALDWYN** stops. The **KING** is looking him with full regal intensity dead in the eye.)*

BALDWYN. *(Suddenly uncertain.)* You're...not...are...you?

KING. Got you again, Anthony! My word! If I looked up the word "gullible" there would be an etching of you, I swear!

BALDWYN. Well, you know what they say...

KING. No, what do they say?

*(**BALDWYN** flounders.)*

KING. "If you stand for nothing, you'll fall for anything!" That's what Little Joan used to say. Whatever happened to her?

(Fanfare.)

O, that's my cue!

BALDWYN. Wait, your majesty, the papers!

KING. *(Signing.)* Next time, I want a copy to study before signing!

(**KING** *exits to balcony.*)

BALDWYN. He hasn't touched his tea! Make him drink! And double his dose, dammit!

SIMPKINS. *(Checking the bottle.)* The bottle said one drop a day, sir. Anymore and he'd be –

BALDWYN. A jabbering idiot? Fine! Anything is better than a king with a mind of his own!

(The Archery Contest begins.)

(Pomp. Banners. Colour. Music. Roast deer. Free beer. As much bustle as can be mustered. **VILLAGERS** *enter and gather with their bows and arrows, eager and hopefully that they might win. They eye the big target that's brought in.* **SIMPKINS** *whips up the* **CROWD** *by placing a large bag of coins on a plinth up on high. The cash prize.* **BALDWYN** *and* **MARIAN** *on balcony.* **BALDWYN** *looks on edge. The* **KING** *is up there too.)*

SIMPKINS. Step right up and display your bowmanship. Anyone can try their hand, regardless of class, creed or economic background. See if you can hit the bull in the eye! The winner is whoever can pull off the impossible by splitting the arrow shaft right down the centre! Who will win?

(Suddenly, stirring strings (Hans Zimmerish) swell as **ROBIN HOOD 2** *enters in action movie slo-mo. He's the broad, grizzled, weird-haired Alpha Russell Crowe-ish version.)*

ROBIN HOOD 2. *(To **ROBIN HOOD 1**, who watches on in horror.)* Sign me up for this tournament and I'll pay you a penny for carrying my bow.

ROBIN HOOD 1. What fresh hell is this?

JENNY. *(Stands in front of **ROBIN HOOD 2**.)* O no! No, no, no! I'm very sorry but we can't have you here!

ROBIN HOOD 1. Yes man, I was here first.

ROBIN HOOD 2. And what fever-brained child's idea of a pantomime did you skip from, friend?

ROBIN HOOD 1. And what wildly unrecognisable accent do you speak with, friend?

ROBIN HOOD 2. *(Growls.)* I hail from the North of England. But spent some formative years in Ireland. But my mother was French Canadian but – NO MATTER! WE FIGHT!

(They start scraping.)

JENNY. No, we don't fight! Not here! Not now! Come on! Off!

(She ushers them off.)

SIMPKINS. *(To the **CROWD**.)* O'right! Form an orderly queue, England! And let the contest begin!

*(The **CROWD** cheer.)*

BALDWYN. This will draw the worm from the woodwork...

MARIAN. What sort of man are we looking for?

BALDWYN. I only caught a glimpse but...he's a lofty fellow. Probably about your height. Broad shouldered. With forearms that would shame a blacksmith.

> *(**MARIAN** frowns, pulls at her sleeves and stares out. The **KING** waves. The **VILLAGERS** cheer.)*

That's it. Wave away you silly old fool.

> (*The first of the* **VILLAGERS** *steps up. Meanwhile,* **BALDWYN** *surveys the* **CROWD**. *They start to shoot arrows that land well away from the bullseye.*)

MARIAN. I take it your men have orders to shoot Hood on-sight?

BALDWYN. They did, but I've changed my mind. I want him captured. I want to look him in the eye as I slice off his bow-fingers. I want to see him scream as I skewer with white-hot irons his pretty eyeballs until they sizzle and slide down his cheeks like fried eggs. And then I shall watch as he dances his last jig at the end of my rope! And then I shall behead him, and quarter him, and place each part of his accursed body at the four corners of the kingdom, where he will remain a rotting reminder to those who dare to question my authority!

> (*Beat.*)

Forgive me, my love. There I go again, banging on about work. Let's just have a good time!

MARIAN. Yes! Let's!

> (**MARIAN** *spits out her drink and ducks down when she sees* **WOODNUT** *and* **WILL** *enter the tournament in hoods.* **WOODNUT** *has her bow with her.*)

(*To herself.*) What are you two doing?

BALDWYN. What, dear?

MARIAN. Nothing, dear.

JENNY. You're not supposed to be here!

WILL. (*Looking over.*) There's the damned sheriff.

WOODNUT. (*Darkly.*) Yes. There he is...

WILL. What I wouldn't give for two new bow-fingers. Straight through the heart. Fffftt!!!

BALDWYN. Something the matter, dear?

MARIAN. Too much beer, dear. I'll be right back. Don't catch Hood without me.

> (**MARIAN**'s charming smile instantly drops as she exits –)

WILL. And there's the King of bloody England 'isself. Which one you gonna go for? Ha!

WOODNUT. The sheriff, Will. I just want the sheriff.

> (**WOODNUT**'s eyes are transfixed on **BALDWYN**. Enter **MARIAN** as **HOOD** from the castle with bow and quiver.)

BETTY. *(Whistles.)* Oi! Kind Hood. You'll be captured in seconds lookin like that.

MARIAN. Shit!

BETTY. Take my shawl and keep yer head down.

MARIAN/HOOD. Thank you, old woman.

BETTY. The name's Betty.

MARIAN/HOOD. Thank you, Betty.

> (**MARIAN/HOOD**, *disguised under a shawl, slowly limps off towards* **WOODNUT** *and* **WILL**.)

WILL. Away, old beggar woman. We've nothin for yaaa-*aahhhhhhh!!!!*

> (*The old beggar woman twists* **WILL**'s *ear.* **JENNY** *is here too.*)

MARIAN/HOOD. I told you both to stay away.

WOODNUT. What are you doing here?

MARIAN/HOOD. Place is crawling with the sheriff's men. You need to leave right now.

WOODNUT. Not until – *(Defiantly.)* Until I've had my shot.

> (**MARIAN** *looks at the target.*)

MARIAN/HOOD. You won't hit it.

WOODNUT. You shoulda taught me then!

WILL. More to Woodnut's point, what are you doin ere?

MARIAN. *(To **WILL**.)* Me? I'm…undercover. Trying to glean information. You're in big trouble, Will. You're in the lion's den here.

BALDWYN. Simpkins, have you seen my wife?

SIMPKINS. *(Calling out to the **CROWD**.)* Lady Marian? Lady Marian!

> (**HOOD/MARIAN** *turns, hiding from* **SIMPKINS** *whilst trying not to act suspicious to* **WOODNUT**. *They're at the front of the queue.*)

WILL. *(Stepping back.)* You're up.

WOODNUT. *(To **MARIAN**.)* Please? One shot?

JENNY. You don't listen, daughter!

SIMPKINS. Next!

> (**WOODNUT** *stares at* **MARIAN**, *who finally relents.*)

HOOD/MARIAN. Do exactly as I say.

WOODNUT. Yes!

HOOD/MARIAN. Keep your eyes on the target.

BALDWYN. *(On a megaphone.)* Marian? Marian!

WILL. *(To **CROWD**.)* If the rumours are true, she's probably passed out in the stables from too much grog!

> *(**CROWD** laugh.)*

WOODNUT. Trying to focus. Shut up Will.

HOOD/MARIAN. Yes, shut up Will.

> *(**WILL** wanders off and joins **BETTY** and a **CROWD** of on-lookers.)*

*(To **WOODNUT**.)* Hold the bow in your left hand...take an arrow and find the notch at the end of the shaft... no, the feathered end!

WOODNUT. Ugh. I'm nervous.

HOOD/MARIAN. Concentrate. First two fingers on your right-hand pinch both the arrow and the bow string itself...lift the bow, straighten the left arm, right elbow up!

JENNY. Woodnut, don't do this! Just get out of here!

HOOD/MARIAN. Steady and firm, wide stance, strong grip, stand side on –

WOODNUT. Like this?

HOOD/MARIAN. No one else exists...

> *(Over to **WILL**, who's joined the cheering. The cheering **CROWD** fawning for the **KING**.)*

VILLAGER. Thank you for the deer and beer, your majesty!

WILL. Don't thank him. You paid for this, friend.

VILLAGER. Did I?

WILL. With your taxes. They live off the money we pay 'em. And they call us the lower class! I'm sick of it!

VILLAGERS. Yeh! We're sick of it too!

BETTY. Then let's do something about it! Come on! To the king!

*(They march off towards the **KING**'s tower as –)*

BALDWYN. *(On the megaphone.)* Simpkins, I'm starting to get concerned! Search the grounds!

SIMPKINS. Right away sir, just waiting for one last contender! Hurry up!

VILLAGERS. Your majesty! Your majesty!

KING. O! Hello, down there! Enjoying the free beer?

BETTY. Your taxes cripple us and we get nothing in return! The system's broke! It only seeks to serve the rich!

WILL. Go on, Betty!

KING. But I thought the taxes were paying for that nice, new road!

BETTY. You're having a laff, ain't ya?

SIMPKINS. O'right! Get back! Mum?!

JENNY. The first move, the first threat

The heart starts to hammer –

SIMPKINS. Get back, mum!

BETTY. We're entitled to have our say, Sandra!

BALDWYN. *(Megaphone.)* Disperse! Disperse!

KING. It's alright, Anthony. The good people were just explaining –

BALDWYN. Come away, Your Majesty!

KING. We were having a discussion about –

BALDWYN. This crowd is becoming unruly.

KING. No! Wait!

(The **KING** *is bundled off.)*

BETTY. We're not being unruly! The taxes are unjust! The forest isn't their land to take!

BALDWYN. Quell this riot before it gets out of hand!

BETTY/VILLAGERS. Riot? Eh?

It's not a –

Wait!

SIMPKINS/SHERIFF'S MEN. Stand down!

Back up!

Easy now!

(The **SHERIFF'S MEN** *draw clubs and swords. The* **VILLAGERS** *gasp then instantly retaliate by holding aloft their bows and arrows. The* **SHERIFF'S MEN** *bristle. Suddenly it's escalated to a potentially explosive stand-off.)*

WILL. Now this is more like it!

HOOD/MARIAN. *(To* **WOODNUT.***)* There's nothing but you, the arrow, the target...wind speed is good...hold...

WOODNUT. *(Trembling with tension.)* Can I let it go now?

HOOD/MARIAN. *Breathe...*

BETTY. Hold your ground!

BALDWYN. Crush the aggressors before it gets out of hand!

SIMPKINS/SHERIFF'S MEN. *(To* **VILLAGERS.***)* Drop your weapons!

BETTY/VILLAGERS. You drop yours!

SIMPKINS/SHERIFF'S MEN. Stand down!

BETTY/VILLAGERS. Hold your ground!

HOOD/MARIAN. *(To* **WOODNUT.***)* Feel the tension in the wood of the bow...the string is singing...the angle of your body, strong, anchored, braced like an oak against the storm... Breathe...*annnnnnnd*...release!

>   *(***WOODNUT*** fires – FFFFFTTT!!! DRRRRGG!!!)*

SIMPKINS. Bull's eye!

>   *(Everyone stops and cheers.)*

WOODNUT. Thanks. Think I got the hang of it now.

>   *(***WOODNUT*** takes another arrow, draws, then suddenly turns and aims at ***BALDWYN***. She releases with a cry of vengeance –)*

MARIAN. No!

>   *(***MARIAN*** shoves her and the arrow goes slightly wide – FFFTTT!!! – it flies through the air and embeds an inch above ***BALDWYN****'s head. He screams.)*

HOOD/MARIAN. Husband!

WOODNUT. What?

HOOD/MARIAN. I mean –

SIMPKINS. You! Child! You intentionally aimed for the sheriff!

JENNY. They'll hang her for this.

HOOD/MARIAN/OLD BEGGAR. It wasn't the child! It was me!

BALDWYN. Bring me that child!

BETTY. Prepare to charge!

SIMPKINS. Mum, please!

BOTH SIDES. *ATTACKKKKKK!!!!!!*

> *(All hell is about to break loose when **HOOD/MARIAN** fires an arrow herself. It is an arrow that slows time. Everyone stares as it spins slowly, slowly through space, hurtling under noses, over ducking heads, towards the target – where it hits the central arrow and splits the shaft in two with a – resounding CRAACKK! Everyone freezes. **WOODNUT** stares at **HOOD/MARIAN**. From all over the contest, whispers of "It's Hood...he's here to protect us...".)*

HOOD/MARIAN. Run.

WOODNUT. You lied to me.

HOOD/MARIAN. Woodnut, *please*... Go.

BALDWYN. You there! Old Beggar! What a shot. You split the arrow straight down the shaft! Never seen anything like it! Come and claim your prize. You're clearly the finest bowman in the –

> *(Suddenly.)*

IT'S HOOD!!!

> *(Chaos. **WILL** throws the prize money into air. **WOODNUT** and **HOOD/MARIAN** run in different directions.)*

> *(The **SHERIFF'S MEN** chase **HOOD/MARIAN** into the **CROWD**. There's a beat, then they reappear, hauling her out again. She struggles, her disguise still very much in place. But...she's caught! **BALDWYN** skips into the space.)*

BALDWYN. We have him! We have Hood, at last! And now, finally, we can bring this fiasco to an end and reveal just who this troublemaker really is –

*(**BALDWYN** grabs her hood.)*

Behold, the true face of this ridiculous, robbing Hood!

*(A huge collective intake of breath as **BALDWYN** goes to reveal **MARIAN** when –)*

JENNY. Stop!

(Everyone freezes.)

(To us.) I need a minute to think about how she gets out of this. Go have a drink.

(Interval.)

PART TWO

(And we're back –)

JENNY. Welcome back! I've figured it out!

*(**BALDWYN** grabs her hood.)*

BALDWYN. Behold, the true face of this ridiculous, robbing Hood!

*(A huge collective intake of breath as **BALDWYN** goes to reveal not **MARIAN** but **BETTY**! The **VILLAGERS** gasp.)*

SIMPKINS. *Mum?!*

BALDWYN. Hood is your mother?!

SIMPKINS. No! She's not!

BETTY. Be good if I was though, eh?

BALDWYN. If she isn't Hood then where is he?

BETTY. We did a switcheroo. Hood escaped. Long Live Hood!

*(**VILLAGERS** cheer.)*

BALDWYN. Silence! This contest is over! Make her talk!

SIMPKINS. Yes sir. Right away, sir.

BETTY. I shan't divulge a thing! You'll hafto kill me!

SIMPKINS. Come on, mum!

*(**SIMPKINS** takes **BETTY** off as **MARIAN** runs in.)*

MARIAN. Husband, are you hurt?

BALDWYN. Where have you been? I was almost assassinated…by Hood!

MARIAN. He was here?

BALDWYN. Right under my nose. In double disguise.

>*(Enter the **BARONS**, looking down from above.)*

BONEWEATHER. Did you catch the fiend?

BALDWYN. My lords, I almost had him. I swear I –

>*(They part to reveal… **GISBURNE**. He examines the arrow shaft split by **MARIAN**'s arrow. He stares down at **BALDWYN**.)*

If I could just –

BRASSWILT. No more excuses, Baldwyn.

BRICKBROKE. Gisburne is in charge now.

GISBURNE. I want this castle locked down. No one in or out. Under any circumstances.

BALDWYN. As you wish, my lord.

>*(**GISBURNE** and **BARONS** exit.)*

MARIAN. There will be a massacre.

BALDWYN. I don't care. Just as long as Gisburne brings Hood to me!

>*(**MARIAN** heads for the forest.)*

Where do you think you're going? You must stay here, for your own safety.

MARIAN. Am I to be a prisoner in my own home?

(**BALDWYN** *shows her to another room. She enters. CLANKK!!* **MARIAN** *paces.* **JENNY** *watches her.*)

JENNY. She doesn't want to be here

Her thoughts are elsewhere

Her mind is on fire

She lied to the child

And beneath, there's an itching

Beware, for to scratch the wound undoes the stitching...

(**MARIAN** *absent-mindedly scratches her arm – the wound made by* **GISBURNE**.)

(*Simultaneously, in* **BALDWYN**'s *quarters –*)

BALDWYN. Curse you, Hood! You've ruined everything! How do you continue to evade me? How?

(*He embraces his mysterious chest.*)

SQUEAKY CREEPY VOICES. Releasssseeee... *Reeeeeleeassseeeee...*

BALDWYN. Not now, my pretties!

SQUEAKY CREEPY VOICES. But Hoood... Hooood... we know...we know things...

(**BALDWYN** *opens it.*)

BALDWYN. What do you know?

SQUEAKY CREEPY VOICES. Marian... Marian... isn't it obvious? She roamsss...

BALDWYN. She roams? She goes off for long periods of time in the forest, yes. Often comes back with leaves in her tousled hair. Dirt under her fingernails. Somewhat breathless...

(Thunderbolt.)

Of course! How could I have been so stupid?

*(Back to **MARIAN**'s locked room –)*

JENNY. She trusted you.

MARIAN. *(To herself.)* I never meant to deceive her.

JENNY. Go to the girl. She needs you.

BALDWYN. Marian, might I have a little word?

(CLANKK-CLUNKK!)

(She enters his quarters.)

MARIAN. A quick one. I need to get out.

BALDWYN. And why is that?

MARIAN. I need some forest air. Greenery. Trees. You know me.

BALDWYN. Once, perhaps, but now? I'm not so sure.

MARIAN. What's that supposed to mean?

SQUEAKY CREEPY VOICES. *(From the chest.)* She'ssss hiding ssssomething...

JENNY. He's hiding something...

*(He picks up the chest and holds it close to him. "Sshhh..." **MARIAN** frowns.)*

BALDWYN. Very well. You can go to the forest, but I insist Simpkins and a troop of my finest guards accompany you – for your own protection.

MARIAN. I don't need Simpkins. I wish to ride alone.

BALDWYN. And you wish to be alone because...?

MARIAN. Once again, you look at me with eyes full of suspicion.

BALDWYN. You're in love with him, aren't you?

MARIAN. In love with him who?

BALDWYN. You're in love with Hood!

> (**MARIAN** *laughs.*)

MARIAN. Whatever drew you to that conclusion?

BALDWYN. Gut instinct. I'm right, aren't? Admit it.

MARIAN. I really have to go.

BALDWYN. Then you don't deny it?

MARIAN. Yes! I do deny it! I am not in love with Hood! There.

BALDWYN. Look me in the eye and say it! O God, it's true isn't it?

MARIAN. I think you need a holiday, husband. I'll be back soon.

> (*He bars her way, the chest clamped in his arms.*)

BALDWYN. Yes! Yes! To the forest you go!

MARIAN. Excuse me –

BALDWYN. Go, then! Go to him!

MARIAN. Out of my way! You and your stupid, secret box!

> (*She yanks the chest, it slips his grasp, the chest flies open and a hundred* **SEVERED FINGERS** *fly out! They scatter the floor, over* **BALDWYN**, *into the audience, everywhere.*)

FINGERS. *Freeeeeee! We're Freeeeeee!*

BALDWYN. My pretties!

JENNY. Are they...fingers?!

MARIAN. *(Staring on in horror.)* O, husband...what have you done?

> (**BALDWYN** *picks them up and carefully puts them back, blowing the fluff of them as he does.*)

BALDWYN. I collect them. A trophy taken from every dissenter who ever broke the king's law. And I will collect your darling Hood's too, mark my words. Each and every finger I will take.

> *(Enter* **GISBURNE.***)*

Ahh, Gisburne. Good. I'll be right with you.

GISBURNE. There are fingers all over the floor.

MARIAN. Husband, this is too cruel...

GISBURNE. *(To* **MARIAN.***)* Your arm is bleeding, my lady.

> *(Indeed, blood seeps from her arm where she's been scratching it.* **GISBURNE** *hands her a kerchief.)*

MARIAN. I must have caught it on something...

GISBURNE. A little pain never hurt anyone. And you know what they say: "To suffer is to ascend."

BALDWYN. Hunt down Hood and bring him to me.

GISBURNE. And in return you will give me full authority and absolute power to do as I wish.

BALDWYN. I shall have to ask the king.

GISBURNE. You must do what you believe is right.

> (**GISBURNE** *hands him back a* **SEVERED FINGER.***)*

MARIAN. Beware, my lord. The barons say this Hood is a ghost, a spirit of the forest...

GISBURNE. He is no ghost. He is just a man. And men *bleed.*

(Bows.)

My lady.

(He takes back the now-bloodied kerchief from **MARIAN***.)*

*(***BALDWYN*** exits leaving* **MARIAN** *alone.)*

JENNY. Turn your back and there's no turning back

Say your goodbyes, watch the bridges burn

Make your decision

Make your decision at last, never to return

(Forest. The hide-out.)

(The gang are all here. **JOAN**, **MARY** *and* **BOB** *listen to* **WILL**. **WOODNUT** *stands apart, dazed.)*

BOB. Baldwyn's wife?!

WILL. What did I tell you?

JOAN. The sheriff's missis! I knew it!

WILL. She tricked us!

MARY. She wanted to help. Poor soul's conflicted. But she's on our side.

BOB. Is she, though?

MARIAN. Yes. I am.

(They turn. She's there.)

Now you know why I had to keep my true identity from you.

WOODNUT. Yeh! If we'd known who you were, we woulda killed ya!

MARIAN. My name is Marian. Wife to the sheriff. I thought I could swim freely between two worlds. But it's impossible. So, I have left that world, and my husband, for good.

WILL. More bloody lies!

MARIAN. I can understand why you might –

WILL. Your husband cut off my fingers! Your husband brands us all as outlaws and the villagers starving. Your husband killed this girl's mother. Do you "understand?" You're not welcome here.

MARIAN. Let me earn your trust again.

WILL. That's the problem with you lot. You don't know how to take "piss off" for an answer.

MARIAN. The archery contest failed. Hood was not caught. So the barons have unleashed the mad knight, Gisburne, to hunt him down.

MARY. He was brought to the abbey after the great war in the North. His lust for blood on the battlefield was legendary. He slaughtered everyone. Everyone. He believed himself the living embodiment of God's Wrath, come to cleanse this world with blood and fire. He'd suffered horrific injuries. Smashed to atoms, he was, and bleeding out. But he refused to die. The barons wanted him kept alive at any cost. We were told to nurse him. We all prayed he would perish. One day, his blood-soaked bed was empty... and we hoped our prayers had been answered...

MARIAN. You know him?

WILL. Sounds like we're gonna need more than cleverness and disguises for him, then.

MARIAN. You know, if you hadn't taken her to the contest we wouldn't be in this mess.

WILL. What, with you revealed as the imposter you are?

MARIAN. I meant well.

BOB. You did it to please yourself.

MARIAN. At first, perhaps –

BOB. It was nothing but thrill-seeking with your band of "the poor."

MARIAN. Then, I confess. Putting on the hood was a thrill –

(**WILL** *snorts.*)

JOAN. Don't snort! Just listen! Tell us everything, Marian. You might as well.

MARIAN. At first, I did it because I was bored. I wanted to tease my husband. I liked being a spanner in the works of his stupid road. I liked shooting arrows in the arses of his men, sent to carve this forest to pieces. I thought I was doing a fine job, but…who was I to do that? Me, up there, thinking you were helpless animals…

WILL. You lot are the bloody animals!

WOODNUT. We're all animals.

MARY. You're right, child. No better. No worse.

MARIAN (*To* **WOODNUT**.) I watched you climb onto the Hanging Post and stand against Baldwyn to save your father – and I wanted to help you. You were right, Will. I could always go home. Eat well. Sleep comfortably. But now, I can't. You must know that I've severed all ties from that world. I'm truly with you now. No more will I sound the horn or hunt the stag or fire a damned flaming arrow for my husband's pleasure!

WILL. You are so up yourself!

WOODNUT. A flaming arrow? What do you mean?

MARIAN. It's nothing. A stupid ritual of his.

WOODNUT. Ritual for what?

MARIAN. To signal the start of a campaign...

>   *(A dawning dread creeps throughout everyone who knows what **MARIAN** does not...)*

WOODNUT. And when was the last time you did this for him?

MARIAN. I signalled to Baldwyn's men to break up the unrest in the village.

WOODNUT. On the night of the blood moon?

MARIAN. Yes... I think it was.

WOODNUT. And how many arrows did you fire that night?

MARIAN. One. It's only ever one.

BOB. It was you... It was YOU!

>   *(**BOB** goes for **MARIAN**. **WOODNUT** stands in her father's way.)*

WOODNUT. No! She's didn't! She couldn't have!

MARIAN. What?

WOODNUT. Baldwyn gave the order to storm the village, right?

MARIAN. Yes.

BOB. But you...you shot the arrow?

MARIAN. Yes. I shot the arrow. Why?

WOODNUT. No, no, no!

>   *(**JENNY** howls. The forest screams. **WOODNUT** runs into the forest.)*

BOB. Daughter, wait!

(**BOB** *chases after her.*)

MARIAN. What have I done?

WILL. You killed her mother.

MARIAN. No, I didn't.

MARY. You shot the arrow, Marian –

MARIAN. That signalled his men to –

JOAN. That found her mother's heart.

MARIAN. Impossible.

MARY. Night of the blood moon? A single flaming arrow?

MARIAN. But I didn't... I mean, if I did it was...an accident...

WILL. Nevertheless, another cracking shot, my lady.

JOAN. Will –

WILL. Not your lucky day, is it? Now you'll truly know what it feels like to have nothing. Hey, *now* she's one of us!

JOAN. That's enough, Will.

WILL. Come on, Joan! Show some gumption! Her husband destroyed our lives!

JENNY. (*To* **MARIAN.**) You took me away from my daughter, my husband, my life.

MARIAN. I can make amends somehow –

WILL. You can sling yer hook. Go on. Go back home to your goose feathers and your roaring fires, Maid Marian.

(**MARIAN** *snaps and draws an arrow and fires it at* **WILL**. *FFTTT!!* **WILL** *goes down.*)

MARY. Bloody hell! You killed him!

MARIAN. Sadly not.

(**WILL** *gets up, clutching the side of his head.*)

WILL. Took my bloody earlobe off! You mad bastard! I got blood all down me jerkin!

MARIAN. I thought you liked the colour of blood, Will! That's why you went to the contest wasn't it? To spill some crimson? Never mind taking Woodnut with you!

WILL. She woulda finally shot an arrow through the sheriff's throat if you hadn't stopped her!

MARIAN. She would've been a murderer aged ten! But what did you care? You just wanted blood. Well, you got it, William Scatlocke. All down yer neck. Bloody Bill. Wild Will. Will bloody Scarlet!

WILL. Actually, that's quite good.

MARIAN. Take it. You can have it.

WILL. But I want the hood.

MARIAN. 'fraid that's mine.

WILL. You can't use it. Not now. Thanks to you, the band is broken!

MARIAN. That's not for you to decide.

MARY. Will's right. We can't continue...not now...

JOAN. Perhaps it's best you do go back, Marian...

MARIAN. I'm not going anywhere. I'm staying to speak to Bob and Woodnut. I'll make it right.

JOAN. Marian. It's over.

WILL. See? I'll have that.

(**WILL** *takes the hood from her. She doesn't stop him.* **WILL** *exits.*)

MARIAN. Well, now. Outlawed by the outlaws.

JOAN. We should go help Bob. Best be gone by the time we return. For your own sake.

MARY. I'm sorry, Marian. That girl thought the world of you.

> (**MARY** and **JOAN** *exit into the woods.* **MARIAN** *moves through the forest and becomes entangled in the roots. She can't move. She hangs hopelessly.*)

> (*Castle.* **KING**'s *chambers.*)

> (**SIMPKINS** *hands* **BALDWYN** *the* **KING**'s *thermos.*)

SIMPKINS. He's double dosed. Third flask today, sir.

BALDWYN. Good.

> (**BALDWYN** *has papers, the Declaration of Purge. He makes the* **KING** *drink his tea.*)

Down the hatch, your majesty. Now, to the matter in hand. It is imperative we remind the people just who is in charge.

KING. *(Drugged.)* O yes…and who's that?

BALDWYN. Good question. Chaos will reign unless we quash their ire and seek out the destructive element hiding in the forest. Outlaws.

KING. But why are the people so angry? Perhaps I should talk to them?

BALDWYN. Not advised, your majesty. You saw what happened at the contest. They hate you.

KING. Hate me?

BALDWYN. They've been brain-washed by Hood. Even Simpkins' mother has succumbed to his nonsense. But then, she is deranged.

KING. I should have been a stronger leader...

BALDWYN. That doesn't matter, your majesty. What does is that these criminals are done away with...

KING. I really don't want to hurt anyone –

BALDWYN. Look, you old fool – just sign the damned thing!

>(**BALDWYN** *grabs the* **KING**'s *hand.*)

KING. Wait! What's going on...? You can't do... I haven't given my permission...! I am the king!

SIMPKINS. Sir! I'm not sure this is the way we should be doing things!

BALDWYN. "We", Simpkins? There is no "we"!

>(*He snatches the papers and exits, leaving the* **KING** *shaken and* **SIMPKINS** *devastated.* **SIMPKINS** *pours his tea away.*)

(*Forest.*)

>(*At* **JENNY**'s *grave,* **WOODNUT** *sits. She sings to herself. "This shady glade..."* **JENNY** *joins in with her.* **JENNY** *tries to comfort her daughter, but cannot.*)

VOICE. (*In the dark. Fearful.*) Hello? Who's there?

>(**WOODNUT** *is silent.*)

VOICE. I heard you singing...sweet songs of the forest...tell me, are you a wood spirit?

WOODNUT. I am not. They don't exist.

VOICE. I heard tell this forest is full of mischievous creatures.

>(**WOODNUT** *is silent.*)

Are you lost? No. You don't sound lost. You sound...full of sorrow.

WOODNUT. Who are you?

VOICE. A lost soul. Hungry and hopeless but looking for someone who can help. Hood.

(*Silence.*)

Do you know what part of these woods he might be found, child? I wish to join him, see?

WOODNUT. I've never seen him. I'm from the village.

(*With growing unease,* **WOODNUT** *makes to leave. Suddenly, the voice that was over the clearing is now right by her – and into the moonlight looms* **GISBURNE**, *who's cloaked to hide his face.*)

JENNY. (*To* **GISBURNE**.) Don't you touch her.

WOODNUT. To be honest, I think he's a bit of a show-off myself. But good luck finding him. I'd best go before my parents realise I'm gone.

GISBURNE. It's dangerous in these woods. There are outlaws everywhere.

BOB. (*In the distance.*) Woodnut? Daughter, where are you...?

(**GISBURNE** *pulls his hood back.*)

WOODNUT. Shit.

JENNY. Run.

(**WOODNUT** *makes a sudden dash away from him, but* **GISBURNE***'s on her in a second.*)

BOB. (*Running in.*) No! Wait! Please...don't!

GISBURNE. Ahh, the miller who escaped death. You know Hood. Bring him here and your daughter lives.

BOB. Yes...very well... I am Hood.

>   (**GISBURNE** *fires a crossbow bolt into* **BOB***'s thigh. BHHT!!!)*

WOODNUT. Dad!

GISBURNE. Do you know who I am?

BOB. *(Through gritted teeth.)* Yes...

GISBURNE. Then you'll know what I'm capable of. *Bring me Hood.*

>   *(The pain is intense.* **BOB** *cannot speak.)*

GISBURNE. Call for your outlaw friends. When they come running, tell them Sir Gisburne will wait with your daughter at the Hanging Post. If Hood does not appear within the hour –

>   (**GISBURNE** *twists* **WOODNUT***'s hair. She screams.* **BOB** *is powerless to do anything.)*

BOB. Yes! Yes! Hood!

GISBURNE. No tricks. No disguises. Just Hood.

WOODNUT. Dad, I'm sorry –

BOB. Woodnut –

>   *(But in a blink of an eye,* **WOODNUT** *and* **GISBURNE** *are gone.)*

JENNY. No!

>   (**MARY** *and* **JOAN** *run in.)*

BOB. Gisburne...he has her...

*(**MARY** looks to **JOAN** with great concern. They tend to him.)*

JENNY. *(Calls into the forest.)* Marian!

JOAN. Can you mend him?

MARY. I've done it before...

BOB. He wants Hood...we have one hour... Marian...find Marian...

JOAN. We'll see to it, Bob. Don't you fret.

JENNY. *(Frustrated.)* For god sake's, somebody help me!

(The strains of Clannad kick in. A hooded figure comes through the misty forest. It is **ROBIN HOOD 3**. *He is chiselled, clean-cut, with long, luscious dark brown hair. This is the Michael Praed version ITV's "Robin of Sherwood" – Robin...the Hooded Man.)*

ROBIN HOOD 3. You called, fair maid?

ROBIN HOOD 1. Not another one?!

ROBIN HOOD 2. Another of us.

JENNY. Haven't you gone yet?

ROBIN HOOD 1. No, I haven't gone, because *I'm* Robin Hood!

(He holds up a programme that he's snatched from an audience member, drawing focus to the title of the show.)

ROBIN HOOD 3. As am I. I am Robin of Loxley.

ROBIN HOOD 2. Aren't we all?

ROBIN HOOD 3. There is a strange sorcery at work this night.

ROBIN HOOD 1. You can say that again.

JENNY. I need to find Marian.

ROBIN HOODS. Marian?!

JENNY. You're no help. *(To the sound operator at the back.)* Cut the f'kin Clannad! You're like me. No one can see you. We're trapped here! We are less than mist. Of no bearing or consequence whatsoever!

(They let her pass.)

ROBIN 3. "Less than mist?"

ROBIN 2. I know...she's really harsh.

(Hanging Post.)

*(**GISBURNE** throws down a shaken **WOODNUT**. **BALDWYN** enters.)*

BALDWYN. This isn't Hood.

GISBURNE. No. It's bait.

*(**WOODNUT** looks up at **BALDWYN**.)*

BALDWYN. *(To **WOODNUT**.)* Hello again, little adder. Not so insolent now, are we?

*(**WOODNUT** stares at him with searing eyes.)*

*(Forest. Back to **MARY** and **BOB** ...)*

BOB. Need some of your healing prayers, Sister Mary...

MARY. You'll need more than that, dear Bob. Bite down on this.

*(**MARY** puts an arrow beneath his teeth and pours a healing powder on his wound. **BOB** winces as it fizzes. **JOAN** enters.)*

Any luck?

JOAN. No sign of her.

BOB. You hafto find Marian...she could plead with the sheriff for Woodnut's release...she's the only one who can save her...

JOAN. She's gone, Bob. Let's get to the hanging post.

>   (**BOB** *is already hobbling off.*)

MARY. We're walking right into the sheriff's hands...

JOAN. We've got to try something! Bob, wait!

>   (*Elsewhere in the forest,* **JENNY** *finds* **MARIAN** *ensnared in the roots.*)

JENNY. What's mine is surely yours

I'm the consequence, you're the cause

And while you take your sweet time to decide

Nature, in her cave, presides

Themes of death and of rebirth

What flies so high comes down to earth

Where in the deep unknown

A seed might be sewn

And, from hopeless fields, new things grow

Or there's but a hole into which all dead things are thrown...

MARIAN. (*Empty.*) And as if by magic, the ground cracked open and swallowed poor Marian. She tumbled down to Hell, caught by the roots of trees which slithered about her and found their way in, under her skin, twined about her bones, broke her open and crucified her...

JENNY. Come on! Pull yourself together! Please! You killed me! The least you could do is help me now!

> (**MARIAN** sees **JENNY** *for the first time. Silence. Despair. Worlds collide.* **JENNY** *breaks* **MARIAN** *free from the roots and hands her back her bow.*)

> (*Village.*)

> (**WILL** *appears, puts the hood up. This is the moment he's been waiting for.*)

WILL. (*From up on high.*) Hello! Ho there! Huzzah!

VILLAGERS. It's Hood! He's here! Can it be?

WILL. Yes. It's me. Tis I. How you all doin?

VILLAGER 1. Thank you for protecting us!

VILLAGER 2. And for the money!

WILL. Think nothing of it.

VILLAGER 2. Who are you under there?

BETTY. Yeh! Who?

WILL. A closely guarded secret… However, perhaps it's time I revealed myself to you all.

> (*The* **VILLAGERS** *gasp as the hood comes back.*)

VILLAGER 3. He's no ghost! He is just a man!

WILL. True. I am just like you. Poor. Hungry. Full of fury.

> (*The* **VILLAGERS** *coo. He nods. He has them. This is great.*)

VILLAGER 2. But who are you really? Where you from?

WILL. O, here and there.

VILLAGER 2. Do you have a name?

WILL. Hood.

VILLAGER 3. But is that your full name, Sir Hood?

WILL. Well, it's... Rrrrrrrogerrr.

VILLAGERS. Roger?

WILL. Roger Hood.

VILLAGERS. *(Not quite sure.)* Roger...

WILL. But – that could be an alias! I slink through the shadows and have many names!

VILLAGER 1. Go on! Do your thing! Fire an arrow into another arrow!

VILLAGERS. Yes! Yes!

WILL. Anyone can do a party piece. It's just practice. Besides, it's my bow's day off!

(Laughter.)

What's important is we got the sheriff and those bastard barons running scared. Hood freaks the flying fudge out of the rich! No more them giving us the fear! Now it's us giving them some!

(Cheers.)

Let's strike back without mercy! Let's show 'em the colour of our rage! Fear not the spilling of their blood! For they've spilled plenty of ours already! Let them taste it in their mouths! Let them see scarlet splashed down their silks! Let them see that Hood is but the beginning of their troubles!

VILLAGERS. *(Whipped up.)* Long live Hood! Long live Hood! Long live Hood!

*(**WILL** is thrilled by the response.)*

*(**MARY**, **JOAN** and **BOB**, bandaged-up and on crutches arrive at –)*

(The Hanging Post.)

(They lurk in the shadows and watch **GISBURNE** *with* **WOODNUT**. **GISBURNE** *draws a knife and puts it to her throat.* **BALDWYN** *appears and stands waiting for* **HOOD**.*)*

MARY. Here we are again, Joan. Attempting an impossible rescue. What've ya got?

JOAN. *(Frozen.)* Uhhhhh...

MARY. Not again?

BOB. Get me up there... My life for hers.

MARY. Gisburne knows you aren't Hood. It can't be you. And with no Marian, it's either me or –

JOAN. It's got to be me.

MARY. Don't be daft, Joan. You've got stage fright.

JOAN. *(Hurt.)* Thanks, Mary.

(Beat.)

Maybe I can play Hood. Maybe I can make them believe.

MARY. You know that whoever goes up there isn't coming back.

JOAN. I know. For one night only, Little Joan is...

MARY. Joany, please don't...

BALDWYN. *(Calling out into the dark.)* Are you there, Hood? Time is almost up!

BOB. Please...do something!

JOAN. I'll get her back, Bob.

MARY. Joan...

(*MARY is a stew of disbelief, heartbreak, immense pride and intense love. She sees **JOAN** in a whole new light. She embraces her. Beat. **JOAN** returns the hug. **JOAN** steels herself to go. Pulls on the hood, takes a step and –* **MARIAN** *pulls her back and signals to be silent.*)

BALDWYN. *(To **WOODNUT**.)* Do you think Hood is coming to save you again?

WOODNUT. I don't rely on anyone these days.

BALDWYN. They get cynical at such a young age, don't they Gisburne?

(*The bell tolls.*)

The hour is up.

(*Silence.* **BALDWYN** *listens, looks about the place...*)

The coward's decided not to come. Very well...

(**GISBURNE** *goes to slit* **WOODNUT***'s throat when – FFFST!! – an arrow streaks by* **BALDWYN** *and* **GISBURNE***'s heads.*)

Just in the nick of time, Hood...reveal yourself man.

HOOD. Why o why does everyone presume Hood's a 'he'?

(**MARIAN** *steps into the light.*)

BALDWYN. Marian?

MARIAN. Yes, husband. It's me. Release her. Now.

BALDWYN. We said no tricks!

MARIAN. I rescued Much the miller from these very gallows. I split the arrow. I robbed the barons blind and gave their riches to the poor. I ignited the spark of rebellion against king, crown…and you.

BALDWYN. These are just words. It doesn't prove a –

> (**MARIAN** *shoots an arrow. FFSTTT!!! Into* **BALDWYN***'s boot. He screams.*)

These were new! So it *is* you. Gisburne, you don't seem too surprised.

MARIAN. He's known for a while.

BALDWYN. *(To* **MARIAN***.) You're* Hood?

> (*He starts to laugh.*)

Forgive me, my dear. You must find my reaction insulting. It's just –

> (*Laughter builds.*)

Of all the people…!

MARIAN. *(Arrow poised.)* Let her go.

> (**GISBURNE** *pulls the knife closer to* **WOODNUT***'s throat.*)

GISBURNE. Ladies first…

> (**MARIAN** *has no option but to slacken the string and drop the bow.* **BALDWYN** *gives a nod to* **GISBURNE** *who lets* **WOODNUT** *free. She passes* **MARIAN***, they catch eyes. It's the briefest of moments but filled with feeling.* **WOODNUT** *runs back to her to father.*)

MARIAN. Now that Hood is caught, I want you to promise to leave Woodnut, her family and my friends alone.

BALDWYN. *(Still chuckling.)* Your friends? Any other demands, my love?

MARIAN. Only that my punishment be the swiftest of deaths.

> (**BALDWYN**'s *laughter fades.*)

BALDWYN. Death? O no, my dear. There will be no death. Now that you are returned to me...our life can begin again! Come. Let's go home.

> (*He offers her a way into the castle. The gang watch her go in.* **GISBURNE** *stares at them with a searing rage. Then he exits too.*)

WOODNUT. She's got a plan, hasn't she? Please tell me she has a plan?

> (*Castle.*)

> (**MARIAN** *and* **BALDWYN** *stand before each other, silent.*)

BALDWYN. Nothing to say?

MARIAN. I expected to be put to death. I didn't plan anything beyond that.

BALDWYN. What about a simple apology?

MARIAN. Hood is gone. I am your wife again. Let that be enough.

BALDWYN. But it's not. We cannot simply pick up where we left off, as if nothing's happened.

MARIAN. No. That would be weird.

BALDWYN. If you try to run again, play truant, put on your silly hood, disobey or refuse me in any way, I will have Gisburne hunt down and kill all of your friends.

> (**GISBURNE** *appears from the darkness.*)

Remain compliant, they get to keep their pathetic lives. Do you understand? *Do you understand?*

MARIAN. I do. My lord.

BALDWYN. Why don't you try this on for size?

>*(A lavish dress is revealed.* **MARIAN** *looks at him.)*

Time for the mock summer ball. Everyone is coming. Everyone who's anyone. It is to be a grand celebration.

MARIAN. Of what?

BALDWYN. New beginnings.

>*(Village.)*

>*(***VILLAGERS*** cheer wildly for* **WILL.** *They have a hand-made effigy of the* **KING** *that they kick and stamp on. Enter* **SIMPKINS** *who sees the crazed throng around* **WILL** *and approaches.)*

SIMPKINS. Stop this! Stop this at once! Listen to me!

WILL. Well, well, what have we here? Baldwyn's bodyguard!

>*(The* **VILLAGERS CROWD** *around her.)*

SIMPKINS. You're playing into his hands. This is exactly what Baldwyn wants. Go home. Keep quiet, for your own good.

WILL. You don't get to tell us what to do anymore!

SIMPKINS. I'm trying to – trying to help. I'm –

WILL. We don't need your help. We don't need you at all! What shall we do with her, friends?

VILLAGER. Let's spill some scarlet!

>*(The* **VILLAGERS** *grab* **SIMPKINS** *and pull her into a flailing mob. Knives are drawn)*

WILL. Woah, wait! No knives!

BETTY. Oi! Leave my daughter alone!

(**BETTY** *tries to help but gets pulled in too.*
WILL *panics, tries to break the mob apart, but
the* **VILLAGERS** *have lost control. He looks on
in horror as they chant –)*

WILL. What are you doing? Stop!

VILLAGERS. Scarlet! Scarlet! Scarlet!

(Castle.)

(As the **VILLAGERS** *go crazy below,* **BALDWYN**
watches from above.)

BALDWYN. See what your fun and games have unleashed, my dear? I tried to control them. But chaos reigns. Their blood is on your hands. You really leave me no choice.

(Back to the village –)

(Poor **BETTY**'s *on the floor, powerless to stop
the bloodthirsty mob who throw up a noose
and prepare to hang* **SIMPKINS**.)

(Enter **WOODNUT**, **MARY**, **JOAN** *and* **BOB**
on crutches. **WOODNUT** *runs in front of*
SIMPKINS. **MARY** *and* **JOAN** *too.)*

WOODNUT. Stop! Stop! Stop!

(This breaks the spell. The **CROWD** *stop.)*

What are you doing?

VILLAGER. Hood said we could…

WOODNUT. Hood who?

(They all point to **WILL**. **BETTY** *clips him
round the head.)*

BETTY. You should be ashamed of yourself!

WOODNUT. Hood is gone. No more Hood.

VILLAGER 3. Who he then?

WOODNUT. It's just Will.

JOAN. *(To the* **CROWD***.)* Back away now...back away...

> (**JOAN** *and* **MARY** *help a battered, bleeding* **SIMPKINS** *up.)*

BETTY. You hurt, dear?

SIMPKINS. I'll live, thanks mum. How 'bout you?

> *(***BETTY** *punches the air.)*

WILL. *(To the gang.)* I'm sorry. I'm so sorry. I took the hood cus –

JOAN. We know, Will. But this is no way to be remembered.

WILL. Marian's gonna kill me.

BOB. I don't think you need worry about Marian. She turned herself in.

WILL. Did she?

SIMPKINS. As I was trying to say before I was almost executed...you all must run. He's coming.

WILL. Who is?

SIMPKINS. Gisburne.

MARY. Dear God...

WILL. Why should we trust what you say? You almost hanged me!

SIMPKINS. You almost hanged me too!

WILL. And with bloody good reason!

BETTY. She's seen the error of her ways. Haven't you Sandra? You can trust her now.

SIMPKINS. You outlaws, you're good at hiding in the forest. Take as many from the village as you can.

BOB. And hide? For how long? Gisburne won't stop til we're dead.

MARY. Bob's right. How do we stop him? He's a one-man army hellbent on destruction and all we've got is the forest.

WOODNUT. If mum were here, she'd know what to do. She'd summon the spirits of the wild wood – but properly this time.

BOB. That's it. Jenny will know what to do. Mary, you got any mushroom juice left?

(**MARY** *holds up a small bottle.*)

MARY. What you thinking?

(**BOB** *drinks the lot.*)

BOB. I'm gonna find my wife.

MARY. That's...way more than six drops. You're gonna be straddling worlds, Bob my boy. We need to get underground and fast. Come on you lot!

SIMPKINS. I'll come and find you, mum.

BETTY. Don't worry about me dear. I'll be fine. You look after yerself!

(**MARY** *leads* **BOB** *and* **WILL** *and* **BETTY** *and* **VILLAGERS** *to the forest.*)

WOODNUT. I'm going to rescue Marian.

SIMPKINS. What on earth for?

WOODNUT. She's the only one can stop Gisburne dead. She's Hood.

SIMPKINS. Wait. What?!

WOODNUT. She's one of us. Like you.

SIMPKINS. She's at the Mock Ball. Baldwyn isn't letting her out of his sight.

JOAN. I've played the Mock Ball before. If we can break into the castle, we might stand a chance...

WOODNUT. Great! How do we break into the castle? *(Looks to Simpkins, hopeful.)*

Please, Sandra. Help us?

SIMPKINS. Follow me.

(Castle.)

*(**BALDWYN** and **GISBURNE** come together.)*

BALDWYN. It was not easy to acquire but here, at last, is his majesty's decree... I now give you the authority to proceed with The Purge.

GISBURNE. I shall call it...the *Great* Purge.

BALDWYN. That's good. What will you do?

*(**GISBURNE** starts to lash himself in preparation for the Apocalypse.)*

GISBURNE. I shall light up this darkening world

I shall burn their shadows to ash

I shall rip up their clinging roots

I shall scorch the earth, the trees, the skies

I shall smoke out the buried thieves

I shall choke the songs in their throats

I shall murder their gods before their eyes

I shall wash in their blood and when all is done

I shall dream glorious when dear England's won!

BALDWYN. Yep...that'll do it.

*(**GISBURNE** exits. **MARIAN** enters in the lavish dress.)*

My dear, you look beautiful.

MARIAN. Please just kill me now.

BALDWYN. Not at all, Marian. I need you.

(He presents her with a bow.)

Gisburne is ready. Send him the signal.

MARIAN. I will not.

BALDWYN. It would please me greatly to see you shoot the flaming arrow. Prove your loyalty to me.

MARIAN. Please don't ask me –

BALDWYN. DO IT OR YOUR FRIENDS WILL SUFFER!

MARIAN. You said you'd leave them alone! That they'd be safe from Gisburne!

BALDWYN. If you did exactly as I asked.

MARIAN. Gisburne will slaughter hundreds of innocent people. I will not be a part of it.

BALDWYN. Dousing the flames of dissent sparked by Hood, that's all it is. We've done it before. They just need reminding again... No harm will come to your friends. You have my word.

*(**MARIAN** takes the bow, ignites the arrow tip, pulls back the bowstring, takes careful aim and – FFFTTT-WOOF!! – fires. It arcs through the sky, straight for **GISBURNE**. He catches the arrow in his hand an inch before it embeds in his skull. He studies it, looks to **MARIAN**, then grasps the flame with his hand, extinguishing it.)*

GISBURNE. The Great Purge begins!

BALDWYN. You minx! That is the last arrow you will ever fire!

>*(He grabs her hand and holds it in a lock. He draws a knife.)*

We must clip your wings, my love! I still see some Hood in you!

>*(He goes to cut her bow-fingers off when –)*

>*(Suddenly, **JOAN**, **SIMPKINS** and **WOODNUT** burst in with the **BARONS**. **BALDWYN** and **MARIAN** fly apart. The masked trio lead the party by singing something utterly incongruous. The **BARONS** are having a ball and are dressed in Robin Hood gear.)*

BONEWEATHER. Baldwyn! Ingenious idea, the fancy dress!

BRASSWILT. A perfect guise for the mock summer ball!

BRICKBROKE. And a splendid way to dispel the curse of that devil, Hood!

MARIAN. Why are they all dressed like this?

BALDWYN. It is the mock ball. And this year, what better subject to mock than Hood himself?

>*(**BARONS** noisily mock **HOOD** and laugh.)*

Fear not. They don't know you were him and I will never tell. If they knew it was you, they'd tear you apart. Your little reign of terror left them quite shaken. I shall attend to your pretty fingers later...in the meantime, do have a drink and try to relax.

MARIAN. Yes. I'll have a drink. I'll have all the drinks.

(She knocks back goblet after goblet of wine as **BALDWYN** *joins the* **BARONS**.*)*

(Village.)

*(***GISBURNE*** storms in, ready to kill.)*

GISBURNE. Villagers! Sinners! Show yourselves! Your time of Judgement is come!

(He very quickly grind to a halt. He looks about.)

Where is everyone?

(Back to the ball.)

BARONS. Speech! Speech!

*(***BALDWYN*** takes the stage to cheers and applause.)*

BALDWYN. Hood is dead.

(Cheers.)

Quite a dance he led me on, but rest assured, your road will be built and your land delivered unto you. Order has been restored and it is now safe to be rich again.

BARONS. Mm, mm...

BALDWYN. And so, we celebrate! Let us merrily mock Hood, who so maliciously tried to mock us!

BRICKBROKE. We doubted you Baldwyn...we shouldn't have.

BALDWYN. He was a tricky customer, but I always get my man.

BRASSWILT. I'm sure we could find you a small portion of the forest to call your own.

BALDWYN. Most kind, my lord.

BONEWEATHER. No more complications now, eh?

BALDWYN. If I know Gisburne, by dawn there will be not a single surviving outlaw.

(Laughter.)

MARIAN. But you said he'd –

BALDWYN. The Great Purge has begun! To progress!

BARONS. Progress.

*(They toast as **MARIAN** realises her friends are doomed. She forces her way out of the party room. She runs through the castle. Down corridors. Through chambers. She gets to the balcony and screams into the night. This wakes someone up with a jolt.)*

VOICE. *(In the shadow.)* Who's there?

*(He emerges. It's the **KING**, dressed in a saggy Robin Hood costume.)*

MARIAN. Your majesty! Forgive me, I didn't realise you were –

KING. Asleep? In the corner? Yes, I'm afraid I was. I escaped my room and forgot my way. It's been so long since I was out...

MARIAN. You're on your way to the mock ball?

KING. I was, yes. Even though Baldwyn did his damnedest to dissuade me.

MARIAN. He didn't want you to come?

KING. I think he's trying to protect me. But I'm so lonely up there in the tower. You're his wife, aren't you? Marian?

MARIAN. Yes, your majesty. That's me.

KING. He's a very ambitious young man is Anthony. I do worry about him. Would you like some tea?

(He produces his thermos.)

MARIAN. Why not? It's not every day you get to have tea with the king –

KING. Especially when he's dressed like this. Hood. I liked the sound of him. I know he got Anthony in a fluster and that's always fun to see.

(He winks and hands her a freshly poured cup. She goes to drink but stops.)

MARIAN. What's in this?

KING. No idea whatsoever. But he insists it's good for my digestion.

MARIAN. *(Sniffs.)* Marshmallow… Mary say is best for disguising a more bitter taste…a taste like…

(He goes to sip but she suddenly knocks the cup from his hand.)

KING. Ahh! What? What is it?!

MARIAN. *(Sniffs again.)* Ivory Funnel! Your majesty, Ivory Funnel makes one weak of will, easily led and foggy of mind…

KING. But that's me! I don't think we can blame it on the tea…

MARIAN. Who gives you this brew?

*(Enter **BALDWYN**.)*

BALDWYN. Ah, there you are! My queen…and my king? Your majesty, how did you get out of your room? Here, let me help you back –

KING. No thank you, Anthony. I want to go the party.

BALDWYN. Which would be a huge honour, but I fear you aren't of sound mind –

KING. Nonsense. I've sat here and taken some air with your lovely wife. I feel dandy.

BALDWYN. What about a nice cup of –

KING. My cup is empty, Anthony. I have had my fill. And now, I shall go to the ball.

BALDWYN. Another joke, your majesty?

KING. Do I look like I'm joking, Anthony?

> *(The **KING** stands and hoists his tights. With a steely glint in his eye, he's never looked more serious.)*

*(To **MARION**.)* Lead the way!

(Forest clearing.)

> *(**GISBURNE** steps into the moonlight. It's quiet. Too quiet.)*

GISBURNE. I can smell your vermin scent... I know you're hiding here in the forest somewhere... I will find you...

> *(We see underground too, beneath his feet. Everyone is hiding in the gang's hide-out.)*

BETTY. What we doin down here again?

MARY. Shh! Gisburne's up there. Bob...how's the mushrooms? They kicked in yet?

BOB. Something's happening...there's a tingle...a feeling... ooooo yesssss here is comesssss...

> *(He comes up. The roots pulse. The underground hums. He stands and sees –)*

Jenny?

JENNY. Bob? Can you...?

BOB. I can see you. I can hear you.

> *(Takes her hand.)*

I can feel you.

THREE ROBINS. Hello Bob.

BOB. Hello there.

> *(To **MARY**.)*

Yeh. It's properly kicked in.

BETTY. Who's he talking to?

MARY. His dead wife, Betty.

> *(To **BOB**.)*

Can she help us?

BOB. Jenny, you always said to Woodnut that if ever we were in trouble, we could call up the spirits of the wood just once. Well, Gisburne comes for us...

MARY. Tell her I've heard Gisburne cry out like a child in the night. I know where his terror lies...

JENNY. I can try, Bob, but to cast a spell like this will take immense effort. Do we have enough time?

BOB. We'll find you the time.

> *(To gang.)* We need to stall Gisburne!

WILL. Ha! Shall we toss a coin, Betty?

> *(**BOB** nods to **JENNY**.)*

JENNY. *(To **ROBINS**.)* Boys, get ready!

> *(The once-lost **ROBINS** stand, thrilled and filled with purpose. Above, **GISBURNE** stops,*

having heard something. He listens at the ground. He feels it.)

GISBURNE. I hear you, little worms...

(Ball.)

*(Enter **KING**, **MARIAN** and **BALDWYN**. They sit.)*

MARIAN. *(To Baldwyn.)* Husband, where's your cup? Here.

*(She hands him her goblet...**BALDWYN** is touched.)*

BALDWYN. To us.

(He toasts to her, she toasts back. She watches him drink.)

JOAN. And now, for our show! A tragic ode entitled "Of Myths and Men."

KING. This is going to be good.

BALDWYN. I didn't book this.

KING. Shh!

*(In the forest, **JENNY** prepares to incant the spell. She starts to sing. In the castle, the show begins.)*

JOAN. Long ago, but not that long, this land was all forest...and in the forest lived the creatures of the great, wild wood.

(In the Little Show, they create a wondrous theatrical forest where faerie folk roam.)

JENNY. Ancient is the living wood,

Green remembered forest glade,

But Man is young and did forget

The part already played...

Spirits of the Wild Wood... Hear us!

(Forest. **GISBURNE** *lights a flaming torch and goes to set the place alight when –)*

WILL. Yes. Hello. Sorry. No fires in the forest. Outlaws' rules. Underground.

MARY. We're running out of time, Bob.

BETTY. Where's Will?

Above –

(WILL *approaches* **GISBURNE**.*)*

GISBURNE. And you might you be?

WILL. You will have heard of me... (to) have your head.

(He draws his knife.)

WILL. You will have heard of me, no doubt. I am Will Scarlet. Will Scarlet? No? That's embarrassing. You're out of touch with the modern world, Gisburne. I am a protégé of Hood. Here to fill her boots and continue her great works. Which means, I shall have your head.

GISBURNE. Is that so?

(They begin to fight. It's clear that **WILL** *is no match for the lethal skills of* **GISBURNE**, *but that's not the point. The point is to stall the bastard.)*

(Back at the castle –)

JOAN. But the world of men came and they feared the creatures of the wood, because they foolishly saw themselves not as creatures, but as something greater...

(In the Little Show, the figures of men ride through faerie landscapes, cutting down

the faerie folk and the trees. Soon, the faerie world curls up and dies.)

JENNY. He forgets what Nature told him

The Truth he knew at birth

And now he lives as if he was

A king upon this earth ...

Spirits of the Wild Wood ...Hear us!

> *(**BOB** and **MARY** are now singing with **JENNY**. It accrues a rhythm and a power.)*
>
> *(Above, **WILL** gets slashed by **GISBURNE**'s blade, but is defiant.)*

GISBURNE. Now I know why they call you Scarlet...it seems you're full of it.

WILL. It's a good name though! She came up with it. Pretty bloody memorable, don't ya think?

> *(He goes for **GISBURNE** but gets slashed again.)*

GISBURNE. You really think you will be remembered for your name? You will die in the dirt, forgotten, along with the rest of your kind.

WILL. Guess we'll never know.

GISBURNE. O, I'm sure of it.

> *(BBTTH-DUNKKK!!! Without warning, **GISBURNE** fires an arrow straight into **WILL**'s heart. Everyone stops and hears and feels this. **WILL** sways and smiles at **GISBURNE** –)*

WILL. Remembered not for my name...for what I did... Cus just this once, I did good.

> *(Poor **WILL** sinks down dead.)*

JENNY. He refuses now to see

Those realms before he came,

Of England filled with faerie folk

Here long before his reign

> *(In the Little Show, **WOODNUT** strikes a light and throws it into the faerie forest where it catches fire. Simultaneously, in the forest, **GISBURNE** finally throws a flaming torch into the darkness and suddenly, flames erupt about the trees.)*

GISBURNE. Burn! *Burn!*

JENNY. Men, who feared the ancient wood,

Will smoke the spirits out!

And burn those myths to ashes

And claim themselves devout!

> *(The forest is ablaze.)*

GISBURNE. *(Circling the clearing.)* WELL? WHERE ARE YOU? SHOW YOURSELVES SO THAT I MIGHT STRIKE YOU DOWN WITH ALL FURY! YOUR PRECIOUS WOOD IS ABLAZE! I SHALL SCORCH IT BLACK! BURN IT TO ASH! YOU HAVE NOWHERE LEFT TO HIDE! SHOW YOURSELF! FACE ME!

> *(The forest sighs. The flames die. An eerie hush befalls everything. From the heart of the wood, an other-worldly light shines through as the door to another realm cracks open. In the light, figures appear. The **THREE ROBINS** follow their leader, the Goddess of the Wild, **JENNY**. She is held aloft by the living roots. It seems she is the very forest itself. This terrifies **GISBURNE**.)*

GISBURNE. Where am I?

JENNY. A place of great ancientness

Where the skin between worlds is thin

This place of great ancientness

Where she came to drink Nature in.

> (**GISBURNE** *tries to fire his crossbow at the* **ROBINS**.)

ROBIN 1. Your weapons don't work here, friend.

ROBIN 2. Your rage has no power over us.

ROBIN 3. You are flesh. We are fiction.

ROBINS. We are less than mist!

> (**GISBURNE** *is stripped of his weapons. A strange and ancient dance begins. He tries to escape but cannot.*)

GISBURNE. What are you?

JENNY. I am the Spirit of the Great, Wild Wood and I cannot die.

Time to take your place... in the roots and the earth...

GISBURNE. Noooo!

> (*They suddenly grab him and pull him into the darkness.*)
>
> (*Ball.*)
>
> (*The Little Show has a similar picture of the Goddess centre of the tiny stage.*)

KING. The forest is awake! And it is angry! I'm loving this!

BALDWYN. A little on-the-nose though, eh?

WOODNUT. "I am the Great, Wild Wood and I will never die!"

KING. Bravo!

> *(The **KING** applauds the show. The company bow.)*

JOAN. So, now that the world of men has faded, shall we return to the wild?

SIMPKINS. Let's pack up.

> *(As **JOAN** and **SIMPKINS** gather up their stuff, a masked **WOODNUT** stands before **MARIAN**.)*

WOODNUT. *(Trying to be subtle, but geting increasingly emphatic.)* Marian? Marian. MARIAN! MAA-REE-YON!!!

MARIAN. *(Not getting the message.)* What?

KING. I think they're trying to tell you something.

WOODNUT. *(Grabbing her hand.)* RUN, MARIAN!

MARIAN. Woodnut!

BALDWYN. What?!

> *(All the masks come off. Everyone runs.)*

JOAN. Hello, your majesty!

KING. Joany! I knew it! What a show!

JOAN. How's the old dog-jaw?

> *(They bark at each other joyously.)*

BALDWYN. Stop them!

> *(**JOAN** and the **KING** attack **BALDWYN**, barking at him like a couple of mad dogs.)*

(Outside the Castle. Smoke rolls in from the forest.)

Marian? I warned you...run from me again and I'll –

MARIAN. *(Voice.)* You'll what?

*(**BALDWYN** peers into the shadows, knife drawn.)*

BALDWYN. Why Hood? Why all the disguises? Couldn't we have just talked? Don't you love me?

MARIAN. *(Voice.)* Once, perhaps...but not now. Not after all that you've done.

BALDWYN. But I did all of this...for you.

MARIAN. *(Voice.)* You did it for yourself.

BALDWYN. Marian, I can give you everything! Just come out of the shadows...show yourself!

*(**HOOD** appears. **BALDWYN** freezes.)*

I thought we'd done away with this irritating folk-hero?

*(Another **HOOD** appears. And another. In different places.)*

And what's this?

*(More **HOODS** everywhere.)*

(Disoriented.) Wait...how is this... Marian, where are you?

*(He swings at a **HOOD** with his knife but **HOOD** disappears before he can get there. He shakes his head to clear it.)*

MARIAN. *(Voice, woozy now.)* What's the matter, sheriff? Is your mind a fog? It's the Ivory Funnel... There was some in my goblet and you drank it.

BALDWYN. You poisoned me?

> (**SIMPKINS** *shakes the little bottle at him.*)

SIMPKINS. Taste of your own medicine, sir...

BALDWYN. Simpkins, you back-stabber!

> (*He lunges for her, but* **SIMPKINS** *pulls up her hood and is gone.* **BALDWYN** *looks about him. The forest seems alive. Something is coming from its depths.*)

What's this? More cheap theatrics?

> (*More* **HOODS** *come out of the dark. He swings wildly but catches no one.*)

(*Trying to shake the visions.*) What do you hope to achieve, eh? You cannot rule yourselves! You are born subjects! You live to serve!

HOOD. (*The* **KING**, *materialising out of nowhere.*) Hello Anthony...

> (**BALDWYN** *screams, swipes with his sword, but he's gone.*)

BALDWYN. Senile old fool! I run this kingdom! Not you!

> (**HOODS** *start to glide ominously before him. He grows increasingly disturbed.*)

Keep away from me! This is not nice! This is intimidation, is what this is! Faceless Masses! Nameless Multitudes! Powerless in all but your number!

SEVERED FINGERS. (*Pointing from the open chest.*) Shame... Shame on you...!

BALDWYN. Not you too, my pretties? Please! No!

WOODNUT. We are one, we are all, we are one –

EVERYONE. We are Hood!

*(Suddenly one of the **HOODS** runs straight at him, with a strange out-of-control stagger. **BALDWYN** forces the **HOOD** down to their knees. The hood comes off. It's a terrified **GISBURNE**!)*

GISBURNE. *(Gibbering.)* I saw them! They - they dragged me down

BALDWYN. Stay away from me! I said stay away!

*(In a blind panic, **BALDWYN** stabs **GISBURNE**. He drops to his knees.)*

GISBURNE. They buried me! The trees sang! The roots were ALIVE!

BALDWYN. Shut up! SHUT UP! SHUT UP! SHUT UP!

*(As he says this, he cuts **GISBURNE**'s head off. It drops into **BALDWYN**'s hand.)*

GISBURNE. *It'ssss all true... The forest isss haunted...!*

*(**BALDWYN** screams in terror as **GISBURNE**'s head rolls off.)*

*(**BALDWYN** finally goes mad and flees into the forest, howling. Beat. Then all the hoods come down. It's **MARIAN**, **JOAN**, **MARY**, **SIMPKINS**, **BETTY**, **BOB** and all the **VILLAGERS**. They have brought **WILL**'s body in.)*

WOODNUT. Will!

*(**WOODNUT** goes to him. **MARY** does a little ritual over him. **WOODNUT** kisses his forehead. **WILL** sits up. He's dead. He sees the **ROBINS**. He waves. He sees his bow fingers are back. They beckon for him to join them. He does.)*

KING. *(Looking about him.)* So this is my kingdom? And these are my people?

BETTY. Now, hang on a minute –

(**SIMPKINS** *puts a hand on* **BETTY**'s *shoulder.*)

SIMPKINS. Let him speak, mum.

KING. I see you at last, with unpolluted eyes. You are my kingdom. Without you, I am powerless. I am nothing. I am here to serve you.

WOODNUT. You don't have to serve us. We don't have to serve anyone.

KING. What's your name?

WOODNUT. Woodnut.

KING. Woodnut, I like the cut of your jib. Inspired by your radical yet entirely rational thinking, I hereby abdicate –

BETTY. At last!

KING. But not before making one last decree...to abolish that antiquated system of barons

BARONS. What?!

KING. I hereby reclaim my lost lands. You stole it off me. I stole it from someone else. So it is only right that these forests and fields, these cities and shorelines, and the vast estates that I once called my own, now be made common land for all! That goes for the royal parks, too!

WOODNUT. Imagine that!

KING. You good people should be in charge. I shall form, before I abdicate, a special council. You must protect and defend and seek out injustice. You could be called The Merry... The Merry...

JOAN. That'll do. The Merry!

EVERYONE. The Merry!

*(The **KING** gives **JOAN** his crown.)*

ROBIN HOOD 1. Huzzah!

(Everyone looks at him.)

EVERYONE. Huzzah!

(The Heart of the Forest.)

WOODNUT. And so began a new age

A time of balance, compassion and harmony

Where the world of myth and the world of us mortals

Lived side by side, for a sweet, short time...

> *(**WOODNUT** looks to see **JENNY**, the **ROBINS** and **WILL SCARLET** framed by the forest. They are in the Realm of Myth now. They watch on as **WOODNUT** practices her archery with **MARIAN**. **BOB** shows his new milling apprentice, the **KING**, how to grind flour. **SIMPKINS**, **BETTY** and **JOAN** rehearse a new show.)*

> *(**MARIAN** throws an apple into the air. **WOODNUT** shoots an arrow straight through it. Everyone cheers.)*

MARIAN. There is nothing more I can teach you, Woodnut.

BOB. I think you've outgrown the childish nickname, daughter.

WOODNUT. I like Woodnut. It's what mum called me.

BOB. You can't use it forever.

MARIAN. If you're not called Woodnut, what are you called?

WOODNUT. I'm not saying. I hate it.

MARIAN. Go on.

WOODNUT. Robin. My real name is Robin.

ROBIN 1. Bloody hell!

ROBIN 2. Bloody knew it!

ROBIN 3. Bloody typical!

MARIAN. Robin? That's got a nice ring to it.

*(She hands **WOODNUT** her hood.)*

WOODNUT. I dunno.

(She puts it on.) Yeh. Maybe.

*(**WOODNUT** pulls her hood up, gives us a twinkle, draws an arrow, aims over our heads...)*

WOODNUT. *(Trying on for size.)* Robin... Hood...

FFFFFFTTTTT!!!! – fires it into the future. Here she is at last.

(The legend is about to be rewritten.)

The End

ABOUT THE AUTHOR

Carl Grose's plays include: *Grand Guignol, Superstition Mountain, Gargantua, Horse Piss For Blood, The Kneebone Cadillac* and *49 Donkeys Hanged*. For twenty-six years he worked with the internationally acclaimed Cornish theatre company, Kneehigh, as writer, actor and co-artistic director. Writing for Kneehigh includes: *Tristan & Yseult* (with Anna Maria Murphy), *Hansel & Gretel, The Wild Bride, The Tin Drum* and *Dead Dog In A Suitcase* (and other love songs) – a new Beggar's Opera. Other writing includes: *The Dark Philosophers* and *Never Try This At Home* (Told By An Idiot); *Oedipussy* (Spymonkey); *Wormy Close* (Soho Theatre); *The 13 Midnight Challenges of Angelus Diablo* (RSC) and *The Hartlepool Monkey* (Gyre and Gimble). He also wrote the book and co-lyrics for Bristol Old Vic's West End musical *The Grinning Man*, and *Princess & Peppernose*, a short film directed by Joe Wright.